WINDSOR & ETON IN 50 BUILDINGS

PAUL RABBITTS & ROB ICKINGER

Rob's dedication
To Dorothy and Eric, my parents, with love

First published 2019

Amberley Publishing, The Hill, Stroud
Gloucestershire GL5 4EP

www.amberley-books.com

Copyright © Paul Rabbitts & Rob Ickinger, 2019

The right of Paul Rabbitts & Rob Ickinger to be identified as the Authors of this work has been asserted in accordance with the Copyrights, Designs and Patents Act 1988.

Map contains Ordnance Survey data © Crown copyright and database right [2019]

All rights reserved. No part of this book may be reprinted or reproduced or utilised in any form or by any electronic, mechanical or other means, now known or hereafter invented, including photocopying and recording, or in any information storage or retrieval system, without the permission in writing from the Publishers.

British Library Cataloguing in Publication Data.
A catalogue record for this book is available from the British Library.

ISBN 978 1 4456 9273 9 (print)
ISBN 978 1 4456 9274 6 (ebook)

Typesetting by Aura Technology and Software Services, India.
Printed in Great Britain.

Contents

Map	4
Key	5
Introduction	6
The 50 Buildings	10
Bibliography	95
Acknowledgements	96
About the Authors	96

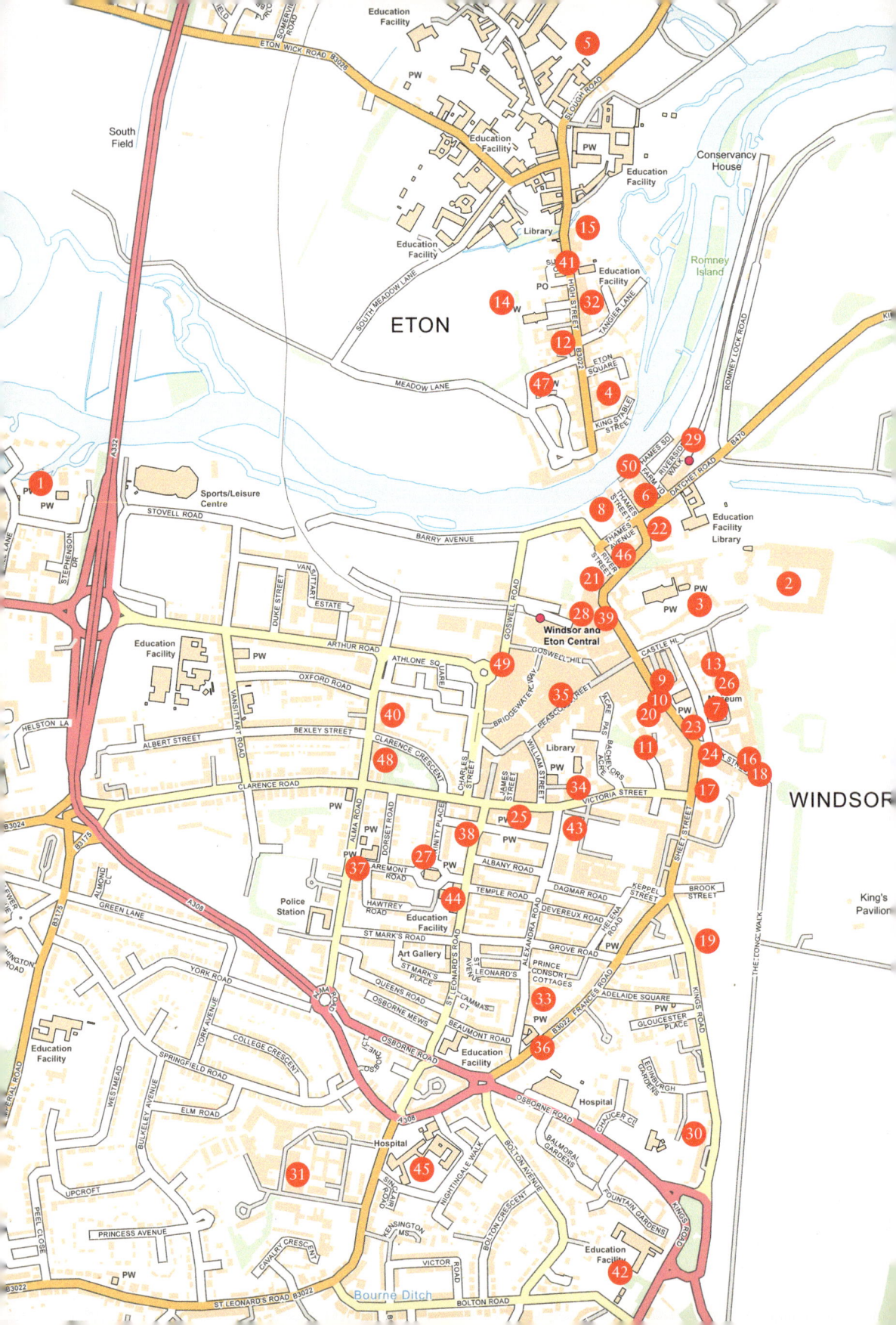

Key

1. Church of St Andrew, Clewer, Windsor
2. Windsor Castle
3. St George's Chapel, Windsor
4. The Cock Pitt Café, Nos 47–49 High Street, Eton
5. Eton College, Eton
6. Bel & the Dragon, Windsor
7. Burford House, Windsor
8. The Old House Hotel (Sir Christopher Wren Hotel), Windsor
9. The Crooked House, Windsor
10. The Town Hall (Guildhall), Windsor
11. Western Cottage and Lychgate, Bachelor's Acre, Windsor
12. The Christopher Inn, Eton
13. Windsor Masonic Hall, Windsor
14. St John the Evangelist Church, Eton
15. Tom Brown Tailors, No. 1 High Street, Eton
16. The Two Brewers Public House, Windsor
17. Hadleigh House, Sheet Street, Windsor
18. Cambridge Gate and the Turret House, Windsor
19. King's Road Terrace, Windsor
20. The Castle Hotel, Windsor
21. Thames Street, Windsor
22. Old Bank House (Brewery Office), Windsor
23. Church of St John the Baptist, Windsor
24. Nos 12–16 Park Street, Windsor
25. Baptist Chapel, Victoria Street, Windsor
26. The Royal Mews, Windsor
27. Holy Trinity Church, Trinity Place, Windsor
28. Windsor and Eton Central
29. Windsor and Eton Riverside
30. Queen's Terrace, King's Road, Windsor
31. Windsor Barracks (Victoria and Combermere)
32. Eton Porny School, No. 29 High Street, Eton
33. Prince Consort Cottages, Windsor
34. Almshouses, Victoria Street, Windsor
35. Peascod Street, Windsor
36. All Saints Church, Windsor
37. Church of St Edward the Confessor, Windsor
38. The Templars Hall, St Leonard's Road, Windsor
39. Harte & Garter Hotel, High Street, Windsor
40. No. 10 Alma Road, Windsor
41. High Street (various), Eton
42. Former Queensmead School, Windsor
43. Nos 67–69 Victoria Street
44. The Old Court and Former Fire Station, Windsor
45. King Edward VII Hospital, Windsor
46. Theatre Royal, Windsor
47. The Church of Our Lady of Sorrows, Eton
48. Ward Royal, Windsor
49. Windsor Central, Windsor
50. Riverside Apartments, Windsor

Introduction

The very early history of the site on which the town of Windsor is now built, and for the period before the building of the castle, is generally not known, although the site was almost certainly settled. The combination of a navigable river and the strategically placed hill point indicate the probability of the area being an area of human settlement from an early time. There is certainly archaeological evidence to support this. The settlement we see today started and grew from Windsor Castle and the fortunes of the town were very much dependent on the castle.

In the eleventh century Windsor was a large royal settlement, assessed in 1086 as the third largest town in Berkshire. However, this settlement was located around 3 miles from the already existing town, at Old Windsor. During the early part of the twelfth century, Henry I relocated the royal household upstream to a recently built, wooden Norman fortress, described in the Domesday Book as Windsor Castle. This castle became the centre for court pageantry, and with the relocation of the Royal Circle, so too did the settlement of 'Old' Windsor, which moved to 'New' Windsor throughout the twelfth century. The first settlement was on the chalk outcrop immediately by the castle gates, but soon expanded south and down towards the riverside.

From the twelfth century onwards, there is reference to a medieval suburb 'Underore', which developed on the banks of the Thames. This suburb was based around the quays and later a bridge built in the thirteenth century. Building materials for the developing town and castle were stored here and the area was a focus of activity.

In the latter part of the twelfth century there began a programme of planning for the new town, which created a number of key buildings such as the parish church, marketplace and a hospital. During this period certain parts of the fortress were rebuilt in stone. At this time, it is thought the road layout still in existence today began to emerge. A bridge was constructed at Windsor and was one of the first on the Thames. This contributed greatly to the growth of the town.

In 1277, Edward I gave Windsor the status of a Free Borough, which gave the town the right to hold its own courts and other related privileges. This helped underpin the town as a significant settlement. Throughout the thirteenth and fourteenth centuries the town prospered due to the close association with the royal household. The castle benefited from repeated investment from monarchs throughout the Middle Ages and this brought an influx of trade and employment for the local population. Under Edward III, in the latter fourteenth century, the castle became the largest individual secular building project of the era, which created many jobs. This was, however, the period of the Black Death, which reduced the town's population by 50 per cent and created a labour shortage, thus royal orders were sent to other parts of the country to bring labourers to the town.

Throughout the fifteenth century the castle continued to flourish and became a popular pilgrimage destination. Pilgrims came to touch the royal shrine of the murdered Henry VI, founder of Eton College. The pilgrims helped boost the economy, and the number of inns increased to provide accommodation for these wealthy patrons. In the fifteenth century Edward IV began the rebuilding of St George's Chapel and this building activity again helped boost the town. Henry VIII utilised the castle as the home of the entire court and contributed further to the building works. During the reign of Queen Elizabeth, there was a flurry of public works within Windsor: the streets leading to the castle were paved in cobblestone and a number of new buildings were erected, including a Market House in 1592. This was later replaced by the existing Guildhall in the seventeenth century.

By the sixteenth century a street pattern had been established. The medieval town was relatively small and grouped around the Market Place. Medieval Windsor was contained within Sheet Street to one end and Windsor Bridge to the other. Norden's survey in 1607 illustrates that the street pattern has altered little since this time, with Peascod Street, Thames Street and High Street all clearly defined.

The Tudor and Stuart era formed a stark contrast to the medieval history of the town. Most accounts of Windsor in the sixteenth and seventeenth century cite poverty, badly made streets and substandard housing. Following the Reformation, Windsor fell into a period of decline. The castle was regarded as old fashioned and shrines to the dead no longer attracted pilgrimages. Indeed, following the Civil War, the castle only escaped the fate of being dismantled by one vote in parliament.

During the English Civil War, despite the long history of co-dependence with the castle, Windsor became the headquarters of the Parliamentarian army. Following the Civil War, Windsor was a garrison town. In 1660, there were 300 soldiers quartered in inns and houses, which exacerbated the issues of overcrowding that the town suffered from.

Charles II made Windsor Castle his summer residence and this did mark the sign of some rejuvenation. Around this period houses within Windsor were extensively rebuilt or refaced. There was a move from medieval half-timber structures to brick. The new Guildhall was built in 1689 and was a symbol of the new, baroque age. Proposals were drawn up to improve the castle and at this time the Long Walk was created.

By the reign of George I and II, the castle had been virtually abandoned as a royal residence, which in turn had implications on the town. Buildings began to encroach on the castle boundaries and the structure itself fell into a state of poor repair. The accession of George III marked a period of renewed growth for the town. Buildings on Park Street were constructed as fine town houses for nobility and remain today as positive examples of Georgian architecture. A theatre was also created on the High Street in 1793. It was during the reign of George IV between, 1820 and 1830, that the castle was to undergo its largest transformation and was completely altered under the supervision of Sir Jeffry Wyatville. The project took over sixteen years but completely altered the castle.

The living standards of many improved in Windsor during the Georgian era; however, by the nineteenth century, there were still large areas of poverty within the town. Windsor was still dependent on a medieval street pattern, and overcrowding, disease and squalor were prevalent. Sanitation was an issue that dominated Victorian Windsor and it is believed that Prince Albert himself died as a result of the town's poor drainage.

The late nineteenth century marked perhaps the most substantial change in the development of the town, with Windsor Castle becoming Queen Victoria's permanent residence. At this time, the queen strove to make the grounds of the castle more private and the Windsor Castle and Town Approaches Act was passed by parliament in 1848. This permitted the closing and rerouting of the old roads, which previously ran through the park from Windsor to Datchet and Old Windsor. These changes allowed the royal family to undertake the enclosure of a large area of parkland to form the private Home Park, with no public roads passing through it.

The queen had a tremendous influence on Windsor's development, as did Prince Albert, who was involved in a number of building activities in the town aimed at creating suitable accommodation for the poor. Being the queen's permanent residence essentially made Windsor Castle the hub of the British Empire, with many European crowned heads of state visiting the castle throughout her reign. The Victorian era witnessed the transformation of the town from a medieval settlement to a modern-day town.

The massive redevelopment resulted in the building of two railway stations, boosting the town's economy. However, redevelopment came at a cost, and much of the medieval fabric of the old town was lost at this time to make way for grander Victorian buildings and street patterns. During this period, Victorian suburbs appeared and development was of a large scale.

Throughout the twentieth century and beyond, the town has witnessed redevelopment and grown to the extent visible today. In the interwar years, Peascod Street was widened, which resulted in the loss of some timber-framed shops to the south. In the 1950s and 1960s, issues of traffic congestion led to a circulation system where Windsor town centre was bypassed. Parts of Victorian Windsor were rebuilt and the town expanded with new residential areas to the west.

In 1979, a major shopping complex known as King Edward Court was opened between Peascod Street and the newly built Ward Royal complex. This was on the site of the former Victorian 'slum'. Between 1950 and 1980 Windsor experienced its largest scale of non-domestic building and the medieval town was completely transformed. 'New Windsor' was officially renamed 'Windsor' in 1974.

As is to be expected due to the history and development of this area, there is a high density of listed buildings, particularly within the castle area and along the High Street, where the majority of buildings are listed for their architectural or historic merit and/or for their value as a group. There are over 130 listed buildings and structures within the central conservation area alone.

There is a huge variation in built form and architecture evident in Windsor, which is due to the evolution of the town over time and the resulting differing styles created. These styles vary from fifteenth-century timber-framed residential properties to large, ornate Victorian public buildings and modern twentieth-century design. Many of these are celebrated within this book.

The 50 Buildings

1. Church of St Andrew, Clewer, Windsor

The Church of St Andrew is possibly the oldest building in Windsor. Rector William Elwell, writing in the 1920s, wrote that the nave of the present church was built around 1100, the north aisle and the tower being added at the end of the century. This is, though, difficult to confirm.

However, the arches and pillars are Norman and the font has been identified as Saxon. This means that the font stood in an earlier building, which was probably a wooden one. Elwell thought that this stood on the site of the present south aisle. Rector Elwell also records that the local tradition was that William the Conquerer

Church of St Andrew, Clewer. (© Ron Baxter)

The 'cosmic' Church of St Andrew, Clewer.

'was accustomed to hear Mass in Clewer Church' – and certainly there would have been no chapel in the simple wooden fortification that he built on Castle Hill.

Clewer existed as a small settlement by the river long before Windsor came into being, with its church, mill (mentioned in Domesday Book) and fisheries. The mill stream provided a safe harbour with access to the Thames. The name Clewer, which appears in old documents as Clyfware and Clyvore, is said to mean 'people of the cliff', the reference being to the bluff on which Windsor Castle stands, which was in the manor of Clewer. The bluff consists of chalk, and this was the building material used for Clewer church.

Occasionally it is said that Clewer church is built on a ley line. Ley lines are said to be lines of cosmic energy that join up ancient sites. Whether this is true or not, it is a fascinating story. Another interesting fact is if you draw a north/south line through Clewer church on a map, the line goes through a tumulus to the north – west of Beaconsfield – and another to the south – by Chobham Common. The suggestion is that Clewer church is on the site of a third tumulus. It was the policy of the early church in this country (under instructions from Rome) to build churches wherever possible on pagan sites so as to 'disinfect' them. The church is also in an area of total flatness and Clewer church stands on a rise in the ground level. This is scarcely noticeable but it was enough, in 1947 when Windsor was flooded, to keep the church dry even though boats were going up and down Mill Lane.

2. Windsor Castle

At the very heart of everything Windsor, on a chalk ridge over 30 metres above the River Thames, looking down over the town stands Windsor Castle. Covering 13 acres, it is one of the official residences of Her Majesty Elizabeth II. It is the largest inhabited castle in the world and the longest occupied palace in Europe.

Originally established by William the Conqueror between 1070 and 1080 as part of a string of defences, it is a distinctive version of the motte (earth mound) and bailey (fenced courtyard) model. It was built to protect London, occupying a natural defensive site in the Thames Valley. The site allowed for one large motte where the round tower stands and two baileys, the Upper Ward and the Lower Ward, the Middle Ward being an extra line of defence. It was Henry I who first had domestic quarters here in 1110 due to its easy access to London and nearby royal hunting forests. Henry II converted the castle into a palace in 1165–71 with a great hall in the Lower Ward to entertain his court and a private residence in the Upper Ward. In 1227 Henry III used stone to build the west wall that you see from Thames Street today including the distinctive Salisbury, Garter and Curfew towers with walls reputed to be 12 feet thick. Curfew Tower still contains the bells used for St George's Chapel and a clock. It was Edward III who transformed the castle into a fortified palace and seat of the new Order of the Garter between

Windsor Castle, established by William the Conqueror.

Windsor Castle at a distance, dominating the skyline with St George's Chapel in the foreground.

1350 and 1370. He Imported stone from Taynton in Oxfordshire and Reigate in Surrey. Raw materials came from as far away as County Durham and he employed 260 masons and a huge army of tradesmen. It cost £50,000 and created the present-day castle's outline.

Over the following centuries there were many additions and alterations. It was Henry VIII who ordered the great gatehouse to replace the public entrance to the Lower Ward that we see today from Castle Hill. Mason Henry Smith was commissioned in 1510 and took six years to complete. Henry VIII gate is more designed for show than defence but provides a spectacular entrance for official visitors to the castle today. During the Civil War, Parliamentarian John Venn captured the castle in 1642 and used it as a prison. In 1648 Charles I was held here and buried in St George's Chapel after his execution. Oliver Cromwell used the castle as an official residence when he was made Lord Protector in 1653.

In 1670 following the restoration, Charles II created a new set of state apartments designed by architect Hugh May with murals and ceiling paintings by artist Antonio Verrio and wood carvings by Grinling Gibbons. Charles II also laid out the Long Walk, the 3-mile avenue finishing in Windsor Great Park at the magnificent copper horse statue of George III. It was George III who began major works to the castle in the early 1800s. Employing renowned architect James Wyatt, he set about rebuilding the castle in the Gothic style. George IV continued this work and was strongly influenced by Sir Charles Long, his chief artistic advisor. In 1824, he began a new programme of works. James Wyatt's nephew Jeffry was awarded the task. He later earned a knighthood and changed his name to Wyatville. Over the following years approximately £1 million was spent creating new royal apartments, including the Waterloo Chamber showing

Windsor Castle. (© Cliff Hope)

portraits commissioned by Sir Thomas Lawrence to commemorate the defeat of Napoleon at the Battle of Waterloo. The round tower was re-cased and heightened and the silhouette of the castle was enhanced by adding extra crenulations, battlements and towers, thus transforming from the medieval castle to the Gothic style we now recognise today.

It was during Queen Victoria's reign in 1845 that the state apartments were first opened to the public. The queen and Prince Albert spent much time at the castle and when Prince Albert died of typhoid here, he was buried in a mausoleum at Frogmore in Windsor Home Park.

On 20 November 1992, a fire broke out in Queen Victoria's private chapel. The fire quickly engulfed the roof spaces, destroying the ceilings of St George's Hall and the Grand Reception Room, and gutting the private chapel, the State Dining Room and the Crimson Drawing Room. The long process of repair and restoration began immediately, guided by a restoration committee chaired by the Duke of Edinburgh. The areas that were most badly damaged, such as St George's Hall, were redesigned in a modern Gothic style, while the other parts were restored to the condition in which George IV had left them. The highly acclaimed restoration work was completed exactly five years after the outbreak of the fire.

Today the Queen uses the castle not only as an official residence but also as a home, where she usually spends the weekends. She is officially in residence over Easter (March to April) at Easter Court and in June for the Service of the Order

King Henry VIII Gate.

of the Garter. Whenever the Queen is in residence you can see the royal standard being flown rather than the Union Flag.

3. St George's Chapel, Windsor

St George's Chapel can be found in the Lower Ward of Windsor Castle. In 1475 during Edward IV's reign, work began under the direction of Richard Beauchamp, Bishop of Salisbury, to build a new chapel and Horseshoe Cloisters, a semicircle of brick and timber homes built for minor canons. St George's Chapel quire was completed by 1484 with a temporary timber roof under the direction of mason Henry Janyns. The nave was added during Henry VII reign and finally the magnificent fan vaulting over the crossing was completed during the reign of Henry VIII in 1528. William Virtue was responsible for much of this vaulting, his last known architectural work. The chapel is considered one of the finest examples of Perpendicular Gothic-style architecture in the country. It is characterised by large windows, tall slender pillars and an overall impression of soaring grace and elegance. The west window is 11 metres high, the third largest in England and contains sixteenth-century glass. The magnificent carved oak choir stalls with the stall plates enamelled with the arms of the Knights of the Garter date to 1478–85.

Today, St George's Chapel is regarded as one of the most beautiful ecclesiastical buildings in England, holding many examples of medieval woodwork and ironwork. The sovereigns stall is still used by the Queen today and dates back to the eighteenth century. The royal tombs and memorials within include those for George V and Queen Mary, Edward IV, Henry VI, Edward VII and Queen Alexandra and the vault of Henry VIII and Charles I. George VI Memorial Chapel is by the north entrance where George VI, Queen Elizabeth (the Queen Mother) and Princess Margaret are interred. It is the spiritual home of the Order of the Garter founded by Edward III in 1348. In modern times the chapel is also famous for being the setting for the marriage of Prince Harry and Meghan Markle on Saturday 19 May 2018.

The lower bailey of Windsor Castle in England. St George's Chapel is on the left and the Round Tower is centre right. (Image by Joseph Nash, published in 1848)

Above: St George's Chapel, Windsor Castle.

Left: St George's Chapel and the funeral of George IV in 1952.

Paul Sandby RA, 1. (1765). St George's Chapel, Windsor, and the entrance to the Singing Men's Cloister.

4. The Cock Pitt Café, Nos 47–49 High Street, Eton

One of the oldest buildings in Eton, the former Cock Pitt Café dates from the fifteenth century when the Cockpit included a knucklebone floor on which cockfights once took place during the seventeenth and eighteenth centuries and were frequently attended by Charles II. Originally the building consisted of three cottages and has undergone a number of uses including an antiques shop, grocer's shop and lived in by the local cobbler. Timber framed, it has recently been restored and renamed St Andrew's Yard and incorporates residential and commercial space. The works were summarised as 'All strip out works have now been completed in the two Medieval half Wealden buildings and they have been stabilised by repairing/replacing the existing structural timbers in accordance with RBWM conservation team … with consultants working through the pre-commencement conditions in order[to] implement the conversion of buildings into the vertical sub-division of the main building fronting the High Street to internally recreate the original two 'half Wealdens.'

It remains one of the most iconic buildings on one of the most picturesque streets in Eton.

Above: An early postcard of the Cock Pitt Café on Eton High Street.

Below: The former Cock Pitt Café, undergoing building refurbishment in 2018–19.

5. Eton College, Eton

Eton was founded in 1440 by Henry VI as 'Kynge's College of Our Ladye of Eton besyde Windesore' to provide free education to seventy poor boys who would then go on to King's College, Cambridge, which he founded in 1441.

When Henry founded the school, he granted it a large number of endowments, but when he was deposed by Edward IV in 1461, the new king removed most of its assets and treasures to St George's Chapel, Windsor, on the other side of the River Thames. Construction of the chapel, originally intended to be slightly over twice its current length, was stopped hurriedly, but by this time the chapel, in its current form, and the lower storeys of the current cloisters, including College Hall, had been completed. With reduced funds, little further building took place until around 1517 when Provost Roger Lupton built the tower that now bears his name together with the range of buildings that now includes Election Hall and Election Chamber.

The earliest records of school life date from the sixteenth century and paint a picture of a regimented and spartan life. Scholars were awakened at 5 a.m., chanted prayers while they dressed, and were at work in Lower School by 6 a.m. All teaching was in Latin and lessons were supervised by 'praepostors', senior boys appointed by the headmaster. There was a single hour of play, though even at that time football appears to have been popular, for a sentence set for Latin translation in 1519 was 'We will play with a bag full of wynde'. Lessons finished at 8 p.m. and there were only two holidays, each three weeks in duration, at Christmas (when the scholars remained at Eton) and in the summer. These holidays divided the school year into two 'halves', a word that has survived despite the change to a three-term year in the eighteenth century.

From the earliest days of the school, the education received by the scholars was shared by others who did not lodge in college, but who lived in the town with a landlady. By the early eighteenth century, the number of such 'Oppidans' (from the Latin '*oppidum*' meaning 'town') had grown to the extent that more formal arrangements were needed, and the first of the 'Dame's Houses', Jourdelay's, was built in 1722. By 1766 there were thirteen houses, and increasingly the responsibility for running them fell to masters as much as to the dame.

The school continued to grow and flourished, particularly under the long reign of George III (1760–1820). George spent much of his time at Windsor, frequently visiting the school and entertaining boys at Windsor Castle. The school in turn made George's birthday, 4 June, into a holiday. Though these celebrations now never fall on that day, Eton's 'Fourth of June', marked by speeches, cricket, a procession of boats and picnics on 'Agar's Plough', remains an important occasion in the school year.

By the middle of the nineteenth century reform was long overdue; the Clarendon Commission of 1861 investigated conditions in the major boarding schools of the day and led to significant changes including improved accommodation, a wider curriculum and better-qualified staff. Numbers continued to grow, and by 1891 there were over 1,000 boys in the school, a figure that grew pretty steadily until the 1970s, by which time the school had reached its present size of around 1,300 boys.

Eton College chapel.

Right: Gargoyle at Eton College of M. R. James, scholar and author of ghost stories. (www.exploretheworld.co.nz/windsor.html)

Below: Eton College with the chapel on the right and the Lupton Tower central.

Above: Eton College and intricate brickwork to the building.

Left: Decorative additions enhancing an important gateway.

Right: Eton College.

Below: Eton College Memorial Buildings, listed as the School Hall and Library. The library holds over 150,000 items ranging from the ninth to the twenty-first century.

Above: The School Hall and Library.

Left: Eton College School Hall, built as a memorial to the Etonians who were killed in the Boer War. It is used today for assemblies and concerts.

6. Bel & the Dragon, Windsor

The Bel & the Dragon on Thames Street is steeped in heritage. This historic restaurant and tearoom has been serving food and drink in this location since the eleventh century.

In the middle of the sixteenth century, Windsor was still a very small town, with its resident population barely a thousand people and its buildings concentrated around the marketplace and along the five main streets. The inns and alehouses were to be found mainly along the High Street and Thames Street (known as Bisshopstrate in the fourteenth and fifteenth centuries). Between the top of Peascod Street and the parish church there were at least six drinking establishments. In Tudor times, alehouses were first licensed under the Licensing Act of 1552. These were then the humblest of the three different types of establishments, often catering for the poorer section of the community, offering cheap food to workmen as well as beer and ale. Taverns were first licensed in 1553 and sold wine, not ale, and some of the taverns were also inns. The main purpose of these inns was to provide guest rooms, stabling and food and drink for travellers. In Tudor times, there was no requirement to be licensed at all. Gradually, however, the alehouse laws were extended to cover inns also. A certificate, drawn up in 1577 by Windsor Magistrates at the request of the government, gives the following numbers for Windsor: eight inns, five taverns and eight alehouses.

The Bel & the Dragon public house.

The Bel & the Dragon has undergone many changes, with the current building probably seventeenth century. The three-gabled building is clearly a stuccoed timber-framed building and has been the South Western Hotel, the William the Fourth and now the Bel & the Dragon. Often referred to as the 'first and last' pub, it was the first one a visitor would see after crossing the bridge from Eton and the last one a condemned man would see on his way to the gallows, which once stood by the bridge itself.

7. Burford House, Windsor

Adjacent to The Royal Mews on St Albans Road you can see part of Burford House. Charles II had it built for his mistress Nell Gwyn in 1678. She rose from an impoverished prostitute and orange seller to become an admired restoration actress when she caught the attention of the king and had two sons by him – Charles and James. Charles II had a strong affection for Windsor so housing his mistress so close to the castle was convenient. She was clearly a strong woman. Legend has it she held her first child out of a window as King Charles passed by and threatened to drop him unless he was given a title. He was to later become the Duke of St Albans. She also insisted on the freehold for Burford House, which she was given in 1680 and her descendants continued to live there until the late eighteenth century. The interiors of

Burford House, although little remains of the original.

the house were decorated by Antonio Verrio and internal woodcarvings created by Grinling Gibbons. Nell died in 1687 but her son Charles, Duke of St Albans. lived there. Apparently much like his father, he was a fine soldier and in great favour with William III. He acted as Lord Lieutenant of Berkshire and went on to marry Diana, the sole heir of Aubery de Vere, last Earl of Oxford. Burford House stayed in the family until 1781 when it was sold to George III.

It is true to say that the Burford House of today is very different to that of 1680. It was radically redesigned in 1842 by architect Edward Blore, who covered the building in stucco, creating castellations and modernising the windows. A lot of the building has not survived but parts are incorporated into the present Burford House. It is, however, fitting that the name of the road it is situated on is derived from Nell's first son.

8. The Old House Hotel (Sir Christopher Wren Hotel), Windsor

The Old House Hotel, now named the Sir Christopher Wren Hotel, close to the River Thames, has courted controversy for over eighty years. A painted inscription dates the building as being built in 1676 and records that Sir Christopher Wren apparently lived here. However, this is highly unlikely and no evidence exists to suggest he ever did. It is known from the minutes of the Corporation of Windsor

Sir Christopher Wren Hotel, although links with the great architect are doubtful.

Town book that Wren rented a building just outside Windsor known as The Mylles, which was close to the town's waterworks. The earliest existing document dates from 1689 and records the minutes of the Corporation of Windsor and, on one page, it states that Windsor's Guild Hall 'should be finished under the direction of Sir Christopher Wren' following the death of the original architect Thomas Fitz.

There is no mention of any other Wren building in Windsor. Likewise, *A Biographical Dictionary of British Architects 1660–1840* by Sir Howard Colvin, who was one of the leading architectural historians of England and wrote his landmark reference book in 1954, makes no reference to any other building in Windsor designed by Wren. A Kelly's Directory of 1899, which lists all the principal monuments of the town, only mentions the Guildhall as having a Wren connection.

Early records show that in 1788 the Old House Hotel was owned originally by the Jervoise family, who had taken the house to be close to their son, who attended Eton College. Formerly the house had been owned by the Cheshire family and during their time, the house had been a very active home full of society and hospitality, until hardship struck with Mr Cheshire suffering money and health problems. The eldest daughter married the future Lord Fauconberg, who regrettably died soon after from a fit of apoplexy.

Following the Jervoises' ownership, the house was owned by the More family, Mr More being the local bargemaster and coal merchant to the king. More opened a gateway that led to a wharf by the river and erected stables for the many horses needed to tow the barges. The More family were more than able to maintain the house to a very high standard.

There is little information on the house in the nineteenth century until 1860 when its ownership seemed to be with a Mr T. A. More, possibly a descendant of the bargemaster and coal merchant. The brick in the bay of the drawing room gives 1752 as the date when the room was likely to have been extended, and when the fine alabaster fireplace attributed to Sir Thomas Fettiplace, *c.* 1442, was fitted.

In the latter part of the nineteenth century, the house was taken by Baroness de Vaux. Her son was often considerably enamored and amused by a ghost in one of the bedrooms. As a result, his mother would not sleep in that room, and each year a number of servants left because of these subsequent rumours. In 1918, the house was empty for a number of years. It was known locally as the haunted house, and it was not unusual then for people to go down the steps towards the Donkey House and behind what is now an office block, rather than venture past it.

In the 1920s two sisters, the Misses Outlaw, ran the house as the Riverholme restaurant and guest house. They were exceptionally popular and were known for their impeccable taste. Mr Ian Black, an Old Etonian, then bought the house and built the present restaurant. He also extended the building by one floor of bedrooms at the rear of the hotel. From 1946 to 1950, the charming Potters owned the hotel and they were followed by James Miers. During his earlier years the hotel thrived and had the enviable reputation as the social centre of Windsor. He built the second floor of bedrooms at the rear. There was a pretty octagonal house at the very end by the bridge, which was a toll house. Unfortunately, this was pulled down. The hotel was then extended by a new wing of bedrooms looking directly over the River Thames and Windsor Bridge.

The Mogford family took over the hotel from 1982 to 1985, the Mogford brothers being second generation hoteliers. It was then bought by Greenstar Hotels plc, who extensively refurbished the hotel. The year 1996 saw the hotel under new ownership and its services and facilities have been increased by the addition of a business centre located within another listed building fronting the river and Windsor Bridge, directly opposite the hotel.

9. The Crooked House, Windsor

One of the most iconic buildings in Windsor is the Crooked House (also known as the Market Cross House) and dates from 1687. The original building in this location was rented by a butcher, with the area once known as the shambles, a meat market for Windsor.

Below left: An Edwardian postcard of the 'Crooked House'.

Below right: The Crooked House, currently a jewellers.

The 'crookedness' is most obvious and this remains an iconic building in Windsor.

The Market Cross House had stood straight and upright for almost 100 years until in 1687 the city council ordered the building to be demolished in order to make room for building the neighbouring Guildhall. A bitter land dispute ensued over the property, and eventually the council gained a court order to rebuild the Market Cross House adjacent and to allow the Guildhall to be built to its present size.

A number of rumours and reasons abound as to why the house is so crooked. One is that it was hastily rebuilt in a careless way with unseasoned green oak and shortly after construction began to warp into a distinctly crooked appearance that has become it's defining feature. Another suggestion is that the lean only appeared after adjoining buildings were demolished in the late 1820s. When these buildings were demolished, the house was left without support and thus began to bend. Supporters of this view also point to an oil painting in the neighbouring Guildhall. During the late Victorian period, the Crooked House of Windsor was a beer shop known as the Royal Standard. The house is depicted in this painting without the tilt that it is so famous for today.

The Crooked House has been used for a variety of businesses over the years. Among other things, the building had been a jeweller's, a gift shop, an antique shop, brewers and beer shop, printers (1931), architects, fruit seller, coal merchant and florists. It was until recently transformed into a tea house and restaurant. This was ever present for thirty years, before it was closed down in 2015 and the house was put up for sale for £ 1.5 million. By October 2016 the doors were finally reopened and it was opened to the public once more as Market Cross House changed use once again. This time as a business selling pearl jewelry.

Of course, one of the more romantic rumours and story is of a tunnel that runs from the basement of the Crooked House into Windsor Castle and was allegedly used by Charles II and Nell Gwynn for secret trysts.

10. The Town Hall (Guildhall), Windsor

There has been a guildhall in the Borough of Windsor from early times. A deed of 1369 refers to the 'gildaule', and a charter of 1439 states that 'pleas happening in the said borough ... shall be pleaded and holden in the guildhall there, before the mayor and bailiffs for the time being'. A map of 1607 indicates a market house in the location of the present guildhall, with the principal part of the building raised on wooden pillars to allow the space beneath to be used as a covered corn market.

The date of the current town hall in the centre of Windsor is uncertain, but was probably built between 1686 and 1689 and was attributed to the architect of St Paul's Cathedral, Sir Christopher Wren. In 1681, there were many reports of fires, with Narcissus Luttrel, a prolific recorder of events, writing 'Windsor Forest is on fire ... this dry weather contributing much to the running and spreading thereof.' There were reports of a 'terrible fire in Windsor, which burned down the inns called Garter and White Hart, and several houses'.

The original Guildhall was described as in 'a ruinous state' and it was decided that it 'was to be pulled down and the materials sold' to make way for a new town hall. On 5 September 1687, Windsor officials paid £1 to entertain 'Mr Clarke's men, masons and bricklayers for a dinner at the first stone setting of the Town Hall'. The building, although attributed to Wren, was started by Sir Thomas Fitz, surveyor of the Cinque Ports, who unfortunately died a few months after works commenced. It was Wren who completed the building.

The new Guildhall was ready by October 1689. However, it was alleged that the authorities were not completely satisfied as they had doubts about its stability and insisted that Wren should support the span of the first floor with additional pillars. This he did, but left a small space between the tops of them and the roof. It was described eventually as having 'a spacious large room, well adapted for the meeting of the mayor and corporation for business of the borough'.

Like many buildings of the time, additions were commonplace, and the town decided to pay tribute to Queen Anne. She supported many enterprises in the town, including subscribing £50 annually to help provide free education to seventy children of poor families. A statue of Queen Anne was placed on the Guildhall north front and on the south front in 1713, and a statue of Prince George of Denmark was presented by Christopher Wren, the son of the architect. The building was eventually extended further by two bays to the east in 1829, repeating the general design of the older part.

In 1829, the building was further extended with the addition of a two-storey building at the back of the existing hall. Further restorations of the building were undertaken in 1851, after the building had been neglected for a number of years,

Above: The Guildhall today and the statue of Queen Anne, erected in 1713.

Below: The Guildhall is one of the most imposing buildings in Windsor. (© Peter Jeffree)

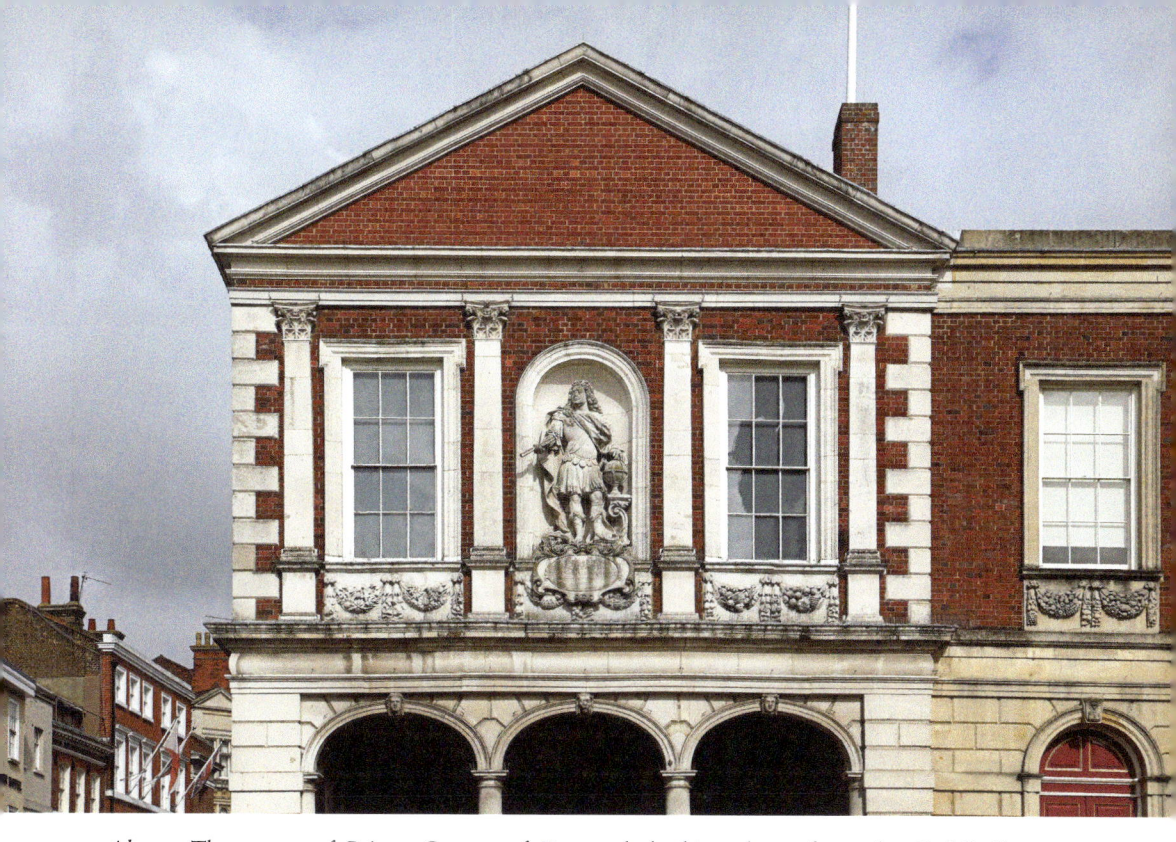

Above: The statue of Prince George of Denmark looking down from the Guildhall. (© Peter Jeffree)

Below: Wren's additional pillars. (© Peter Jeffree)

and again in 1950–51, following its use as a food office during the Second World War. The restored building was reopened during the Festival of Britain by Princess Elizabeth, later Elizabeth II.

The purpose of the building throughout history has varied, with commercial, administrative and judicial all having a role. Since 1974, the building has been used for more ceremonial events including on 9 April 2005, when Charles, the Prince of Wales, married Camilla Parker Bowles and on 21 December 2005 it also hosted one of the first same sex civil partnership ceremonies to be held in England, that of Sir Elton John and David Furnish, who both live near Windsor.

11. Western Cottage and Lychgate, Bachelor's Acre, Windsor

The Western Cottage and adjoining lychgate date back to 1702 and are located next to a disused churchyard. The cottage is charming yet was much altered and refaced between 1850 and 1860. With a mixed stucco-faced and rustic frontage, it is now a holiday cottage. Above the main door is a plaque dedicated in the memory of S. J. Stone, who lived here while he was curate of the parish church between 1863 and 1870. Stone is most commonly associated as the author of the popular hymn 'The Church's One Foundation'.

Western Cottage on Bachelor's Acre.

The lychgate to the adjacent churchyard.

12. The Christopher Inn, Eton

Across the bridge over the Thames lies the small town of Eton. Once a small hamlet, it served the traffic on the road to London.

One of the inns on the High Street in Eton deserving of mention is the Christopher Inn. It was originally across the road from the chapel, towards Barnes Pool Bridge. It dates from the sixteenth century when the inn served a stream of coaches and postchaises, but became a considerable nuisance to the college. One former Etonian, commenting in late Victorian times, said that 'the part which the inn played in the Eton of old, as an agent of demoralisation, can hardly be realised now. Boys were always slinking in to the inn for a drink. If caught, they had been to see friends in London, or to enquire about parcels sent down by coach.' The inn was eventually acquired by the college in 1844, and a new Christopher Inn established down Eton High Street. The current building is a converted coaching inn, dating back to 1711. When first built, the balcony rooms of the current building were used as a magistrates' court.

A great deal was eaten and drunk there, old Etonians lounged over the rails and chaffed the ostlers in the court below, or exchanged a word and a laugh with the beautiful Pipylena, who came to the door of the bar for a breath of air and sunlight; here was old Garraway bustling out to receive the London coach, or discoursing wisely on stable matters to a group of young bucks; here passes a little Colleger with a bowl of 'bishop' [a mixture of rum, red wine, lemon juice, and sugar] — at twelve shillings a bowl — under his gown ... and perhaps you might see what Gladstone used to see from his window at Mrs Shurey's opposite — the prisoners being taken across the archway to the coffee-room, where the magistrates sat — now a pupil-room[classroom].'

Above: The Christopher Inn on Eton High Street.

Left: The attractive frontage of the Christopher Inn.

13. Windsor Masonic Hall, Windsor

At the top of Church Lane, the Masonic Hall is a Grade II listed building and the site of the original Royal Free School in Windsor. In 1705 Queen Anne, concerned by the enormously high levels of illiteracy in the population, persuaded parliament to pass an act to encourage the setting up of free schooling. Schools would be funded locally and were to be known as Royal Free Schools. Windsor Parish Council provided the north-east corner of St John the Baptist churchyard for a suitable school building to be built. A fund was set up to create a school for up to forty boys and thirty girls all with deserving need from the local borough. Each child would be provided with a uniform, food and educational materials. The intention was to raise £700. Despite an initial donation of £50 from Queen Anne, it took the death of Theodore Rendue, the Keeper of their Majesty's Royal Palace, to bequeath £500 in his will in 1724 to raise sufficient funds for the school to be built.

By 1726 the Royal Free School, designed in a bold brick baroque style, was completed and remained as a school until 1862 when, needing larger premises, the Free School merged with the National School to form the New Royal Free School and moved to Batchelor's Acre.

The building was bought by the Castle Lodge of Freemasons, founded in 1859, and after considerable renovations was inducted on 24 November 1864 as the Windsor Castle Lodge where it remains today.

The former Royal Free School, now Windsor Castle Lodge for the Castle Lodge Freemasons.

14. St John the Evangelist Church, Eton

Tucked away off the High Street in Eton is the Church of St John the Evangelist. The earliest history of the church is somewhat obscure. The care of the parish at the time appears to have been in the possession of the monks of Merton Priory in Surrey. It was rumoured that there was a church in King's Stable Street. A church existed later on or very near to the site of the present Eton College Chapel, probably on the south side of the churchyard, as records indicate that this was being used when Henry VI was building his chapel, as early as 1441. In around 1487 this early church was pulled down and from this time onwards, the college chapel served as the parish church, the Provosts of Eton being rectors of the parish, and responsible for the spiritual care of the people of the town.

At this time, parishioners had a right to seats in the antechapel of the college chapel, but this soon became inadequate and sadly the spiritual care of the townspeople became neglected. As a result, a chapel of ease was built in the High Street near the entrance to the present church, at the sole expense of the Revd William Hetherington, a member of the college. This church was consecrated on 8 September 1769 and remained until 1819. In 1819, the provost and fellows rebuilt this small church but on a larger scale. This second chapel of ease stood right on the street, the Parish Watchman's box being against its east wall. It contained galleries and high pews, which faced the pulpit at the west end, so that, except in the communion service, the people turned their backs on the altar. Services were conducted by chaplains of the college.

The nineteenth century witnessed a revival of church life generally. The foundation stone of the current large church building was laid on 21 October 1852 by Prince Albert. Queen Victoria and Prince Albert gave £100 towards its cost. The architect

Below left: St John the Evangelist Church, Eton.

Below right: St John the Evangelist Church and modern extension.

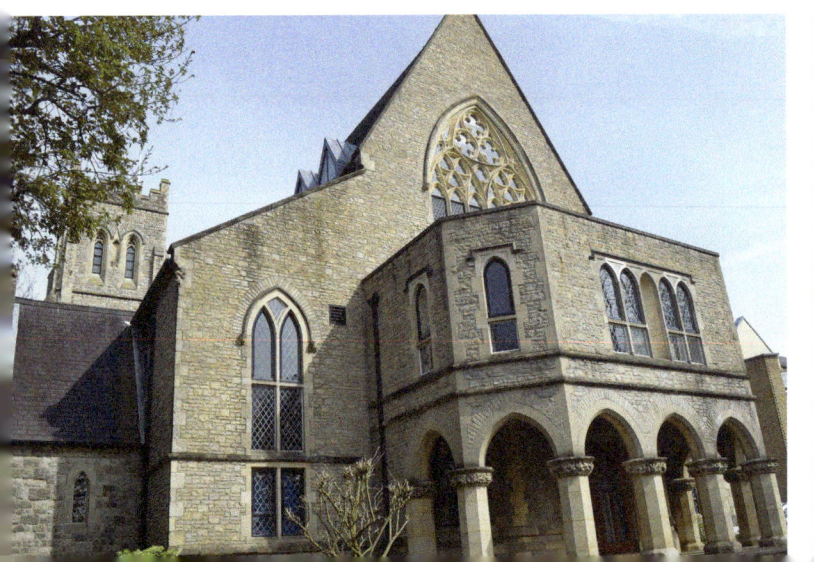

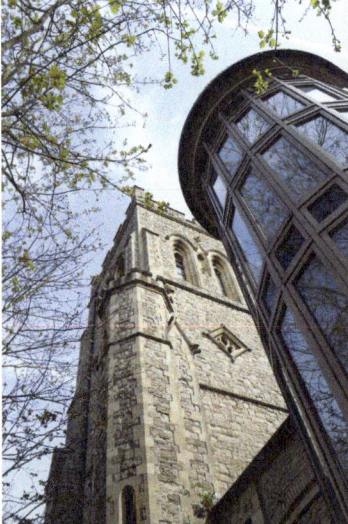

was Mr Benjamin Ferry and the building was constructed to accommodate 1,100 people at a total cost of £10,456.

By 1954 the spire was demolished and eventually rebuilt as a tower. A number of pews were removed from the west end of the old church and the space obtained used to build new vestries. The church attendance suffered a serious decline at that time and the fabric needed a great deal of attention. The cumulative result was that the church was closed for public worship in 1981 and the building was offered for alternative use. Various schemes were considered but the problem of access was a severe limitation. Demolition was a distinct possibility, but thankfully Eton College came forward with a proposal, which resulted in the building use we see today. The nave was completely modified to provide a sanatorium for the school, along with flats for masters and other college employees. The tower was converted to create accommodation for nursing staff. The original sanctuary and chancel have been split horizontally. On the ground floor is the medical centre for the town and on the first floor is the present church. This was rededicated for public worship on 13 September 1991 by the Bishop of Buckingham, the Rt Revd Simon Burrows.

15. Tom Brown Tailors, No. 1 High Street, Eton

Tom Brown Tailors stands at the far end of the High Street at No. 1, closest to the college, and was established in 1784 and remains in the same premises today.

This iconic firm's founder, the first of five successive Tom Browns, is thought to have been practising his tailor's trade in nearby Keats Lane even before taking over this shop on Eton High Street. These well-located premises had previously been used for business purposes for approximately two years before becoming vacant when the tenant ended up in a debtors' jail in Aylesbury. The tailors made clothing exclusively in those very early days for the boys of nearby Eton College, and still continues to do so today.

Today, Tom Brown Tailors is a private company with a branch in London too. The London shop originally opened in 1890 in Conduit Street. Sadly, this shop was destroyed during the Blitz, and the business eventually moved to Princess Street before its latest move to Saville Row. The business is a thriving bespoke tailoring concern at No. 1 High Street and still uses traditional methods including using an old weighing machine, which is still in perfect working order, along with a height scale. Some of the college boys' items of clothing were traditionally changed as they reached a stipulated minimum height – like the now defunct 'bumfreezer' jacket, for instance – so the height scale was constantly in use.

Up until to the First World War customers would initially be met by the proprietor in his formal frock coat. Skilled cutters would also be in the 'front of house', but other staff were not expected to mix with patrons. In the back workrooms these other staff stitched, sewed and pressed on benches, on the floor, wherever they could find working space, with the treadle sewing machines seldom

Above: Tom Brown Tailors, Eton High Street.

Left: Tom Brown Tailors, still supplying the pupils of Eton College today.

idle, and only available warmth coming from the gas heaters of the pressing irons. The treadle is still in use today, as is one of the old-fashioned but still functional iron heaters. One of the workroom staff used to receive an extra 1*d* an hour for answering the speaking tube from the shop. Blowing into the tube produced a whistle at the other end, and the privileged recipient had the extra 'perk' of being able to take the pick of the work orders that came through.

The shop, in its earliest days, was considerably smaller than it is today, with the adjoining premises Holderness the Bakers. It took on its current shape after rebuilding in 1865, and one fitting room has been kept exactly as it was then, still with the original wallpaper, wall prints, mirror and fittings.

16. The Two Brewers Public House, Windsor

The Two Brewers public house is arguably one of the prettiest pubs in Windsor and is a cosy establishment found at the bottom of Park Street by Cambridge Gate and the entrance into the Long Walk. Once the main thoroughfare from Windsor to Old Windsor and beyond to Staines, the original coaching inn on the site on Park Street was the Black Horse, which would have served a busy passing trade of coaches, tradesmen and travellers. The Two Brewers came from the annex of the Black Horse. In 1792 Cornelius Berry was its first tenant. The pub was owned by Windsor Brewery, which was owned by John and Richard Ramsbottom, from whom it is most likely that the pub takes its name. The public house gets

Two Brewers public house at the bottom of Park Street.

mentioned in many local historical records. An example was cited in 1836, when Mr Percy, who was running the pub, was swindled by a Miss Seagrove, who was passing off counterfeit half sovereigns as legal tender. The Two Brewers and the Black Horse both traded until the Black Horse lost its licence in 1869. Apparently regularly frequented by prostitutes, it was accused of being run as a brothel and closed after 160 years of trading.

17. Hadleigh House, Sheet Street, Windsor

Hadleigh House was built in 1793 by William Thomas, an apothecary and later Mayor of Windsor. This impressive house was sold in the early nineteenth century to Mr John O'Reilly, surgeon-apothecary to George III. On O'Reilly's death, Hadleigh House passed to his partner, Henry Brown, who was later appointed surgeon-apothecary to George IV. George IV seemingly became incensed that Brown used the castle driveway, through that part of the Great Park that is today known as the Long Walk, and required him to alter the house so as to have the

Hadleigh House on Sheet Street.

front entrance on Sheet Street. Brown was forced into turning his house around and evidence of this may be seen when studying the back of the house as it is today. Later appointed as surgeon-apothecary to Queen Victoria, Brown died in 1868, leaving the property to his son Henry.

Upon Henry's death in or around 1890, the house was sold to the Leveson Gower family, who were the maternal family of the late Queen Mother. They resided at Hadleigh House for more than thirty years and their family crest appears on the stained-glass window at the top of the first flight to the main staircase. Cuthbert Harold Blakiston, a senior master at Eton College, purchased Hadleigh House from the Leveson Gowers in the early 1920s and upon being appointed headmaster of Lancing College, sold the house to John Millar Watt. Watt was a famous cartoonist, sketching under the name of 'Puck' and whose work was published in *Punch Magazine*. He leased the house to Lady Hazel Macnaughton, whose son, a historian of some note, purchased the house before setting off to war in 1940. He wrote a charming book of the house in wartime, based on the letters his mother sent to him in the field.

In 1959 Hadleigh House was sold on to a development company but within a short time was purchased by local solicitor P. J. Willmett, who ran his legal practice from adjacent premises. He sold the house on to David Bain, a Windsor surgeon. The house was sold in 2015 by Liverpool actress Jean Boht at a selling price of over £3 million.

Turret House, by Cambridge Gate.

18. Cambridge Gate and the Turret House, Windsor

A cluster of buildings at the entrance to the Home Park is of interest due to the variety of buildings in this location. Park Street tapers down towards its narrowest point at Cambridge Gate and this provides a visual focus towards the entrance point to the Home Park. Turret House is probably early nineteenth century and the recasing of an earlier building in this location and is now mostly rendered. It makes an impressive entrance to one of the finest views in Windsor, towards the castle and down the Long Walk.

19. King's Road Terrace, Windsor

A long but plainly built with stock bricks, this terrace on King's Road is impressive due to its size and uniformity. It was built around 1800 and has managed to retain much of its original glazing and doors. Incredibly, despite the loss of so much ironwork to the war effort, much of the original railings remain around the small basement yards, along with the cast-iron balconies, which have a Gothic feel to them. Many of these terraces are now highly sought after and have been sympathetically restored in recent years.

King's Road and one of the many terraces along this road.

20. The Castle Hotel, Windsor

Located on the High Street opposite the Guildhall, the Castle Hotel is one of Windsor's most prestigious hotels. There has been an inn on the site since 1528, offering rooms to the local community serving the Market Square area opposite, which was then Butchers Row, Fish Street, Priest Street and Church Street, today known as Market Street, Church Street, Church Lane and St Albans Street. George Pennington is noted as its steward in 1656, who named it 'the Mermaid Inn'. A bit of a local celebrity at the time, he brewed his own ciders and beers onsite, which proved very popular. Struggling with a countrywide problem, a lack of small coinage, he manufactured his own coins, a half penny token depicting a mermaid that could be used to buy drinks in his inn.

Richard Martin was the proprietor in the 1700s when the Mermaid Inn obtained a royal warrant to provide horses and carriages for the royal household and was the first of eight warrants. Martin was not only the innkeeper but also Windsor's postmaster and a hackney man to the king. In honour of this great distinction it was Martin who renamed the building the Castle Inn.

The Castle Inn prospered during the eighteenth century as Windsor quickly grew and soon became one of the regions grandest hotels frequented by the rich and famous of the day. It is claimed that the Duke of Wellington himself dined here after the Battle of Waterloo.

Above: The Guildhall and Castle Hotel in the background.

Below: The Castle Hotel, opposite the Guildhall, one of Windsor's finest hotels.

The building we see today was built in the early nineteenth century. The beautiful cast-iron balcony is a decorative pattern called 'heart and honeysuckle' beneath a 'vitruvian scroll', a popular design used on verandas and balconies at the time.

21. Thames Street, Windsor

Thames Street was formerly known as Bishop's Street and curved its way down past the castle to a bridge over the river that may have replaced a ford as early as 1172. Although the river played an important part in the life of the town, the name Thames Street was not used until late in the eighteenth century. In the fourteenth and fifteenth centuries, it was called Bisshopstrate and it has been suggested that the name came from Bishop's Tower, as the Salisbury Tower was called in the thirteenth century. Above many of the modern shop frontages on Thames Street today, the windows and rooflines reveal that there are many old timber-framed buildings still in Thames Street.

Below left: Thames Street, and one of the many unusual buildings along this important street.

Below right: Edward VII was a popular monarch and his bust sits in the Olde King & Castle on Thames Street, built in 1917.

22. Old Bank House (Brewery Office), Windsor

Built around 1813 at the foot of Thames Street is Old Bank House. For many centuries, there had been a brewery in Datchet Lane, and in 1786 Henry Isherwood, the owner, sold it to the Ramsbottom family for £70,000. It was there that the Queen's or Windsor Ale was brewed, the firm combining brewing with banking under the name of Ramsbottom and Baverstock. Shortly before his death at Bath in 1813, Richard Ramsbottom, who had been elected in 1806 as one of the borough's Members of Parliament, built for himself a fine new house, which is now known as Old Bank House. In the same year, the house was offered for sale and was described as 'recently and most substantially built … containing ten good bed chambers, handsome dining and drawing rooms, breakfast parlour and music room or library, together with a neat Walled Garden or Lawn, Coach-House, Stabling etc'. Unfortunately, the house was not sold and it passed in 1837 with the whole firm, when it was bought for £75,000 by Nevile Reid & Co., who continued the joint business of brewing and banking.

Now a listed building, it is one of Windsor's finest Georgian buildings. It was originally hemmed in on either side by brewery houses, but at the rear, rose the walls and chimneys of the brewhouse. Today the building stands isolated and is now St George's School, a co-educational independent preparatory school.

Old Bank House, now St George's School.

Overlooked by the castle, St George's School is now a listed building.

23. Church of St John the Baptist, Windsor

The official parish church of Windsor is found on the High Street, not too far away from the castle, and is dedicated to St John the Baptist. The first church here was in existence by the early twelfth century. By the early nineteenth century, the early medieval building was described as 'a spacious, ancient, but ill-built fabric'. It consisted of a nave, chancel and aisles, each under a separate gable. Early repairs did little to improve matters and the condition of the building at the time led to a proposal in 1881 to rebuild and the work was carried out in 1820–22 under the little-known architect Charles Hollis. Hollis had already exhibited architectural designs at the Royal Academy in 1801–03 but after this no further references to him have been found until 1820 when his designs for rebuilding Windsor parish church were accepted. The better-known architect Jeffry Wyattville was also involved with this scheme, but only as a consultant. The church was eventually completed in 1822 and consecrated on 22 June by the Bishop of Salisbury. Hollis was also responsible for designing Windsor Bridge, consisting of three arches of iron, in 1822–24, and the classical Church of All Saints, Poplar, with its parsonage house, in 1821–23. In the 1820s he was working in practice from various London addresses but his name then disappears from the London directories with his death in or around 1830. Following Hollis was Samuel Sanders Teulon (1812–73), who was a well-known and active church architect who worked primarily for Low Church clients. His work is often made striking by the use of structural polychromy and exotic architectural details, as here at St John's, one of his very late works.

St John's Church is therefore the product of two very different nineteenth-century schemes by two very different architects, one Georgian and one High Victorian. The *c.* 1820 church, with box pews and lack of a sizable chancel, was everything that Victorian clergymen and architects came to dislike, hence the thorough remodelling in around 1870 by Teulon. Teulon himself was noted for these radical Gothic 'recastings' of churches and the result here is a somewhat harsh juxtaposition of two very different aesthetics. Nevertheless, a fine building remains to this today with a number of principal fixtures including low screens allegedly carved by Grinling Gibbons for the chapel at Windsor Castle where he was paid for work in 1680–82. This screenwork was given to St John's by George III.

The Church of St John the Baptist is the official church of Windsor.

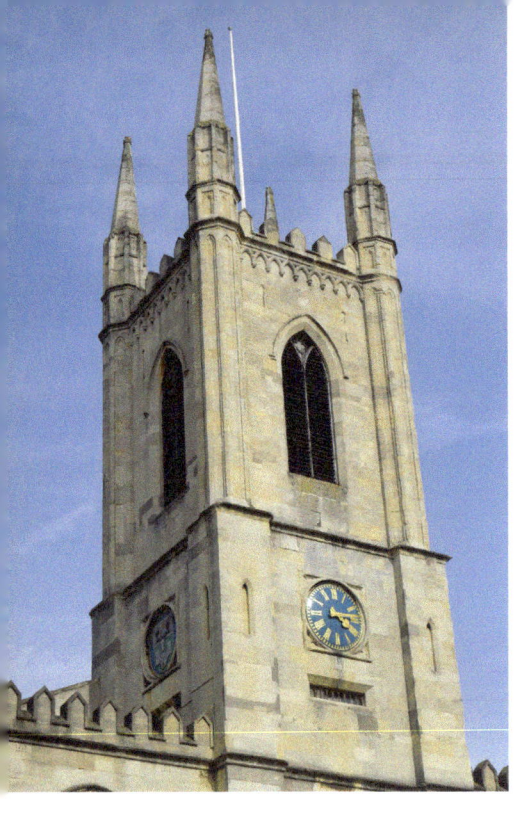

The Church of St John the Baptist.

24. Nos 12–16 Park Street, Windsor

Until the middle of the nineteenth century, Park Street was an important thoroughfare and formed part of the road to London via Frogmore and Staines. The name has changed a number of times and it was originally called More Street, often assumed to have originated from the medieval name of Mor or More Strate, first mentioned in 1315, and may have been a reference to the 'mor', meaning 'marsh', at Frogmore House. It is more likely to have referred to the family of de la More, who had property here in the thirteenth century. By 1583 the street was called Cuthorse Well Street in a deed dated from that time. Its next name was Pound Street, which first appears in the Chamberlain's Accounts of 1653 with 'rent of Mr Baker in Pound Street for the ground where the pound did stand'. Three houses were built on the site of the old pound (the local lock-up), Nos 10, 11 and 12, in what was now called Park Street in the nineteenth century with the 1795 lease referring to 'Moore Street, lately Pound Street, now Park Street'.

In 1826, builder Robert Tebbott acquired the site of No. 12 Park Street from a family of London-based grocers called Hill, the heirs of Adam Hill, described as 'late of New Windsor, gentleman'. The latter had died in 1820 and this was part of a wider plan of Tebbott to acquire further properties on Park Street, where he intended to build Regency-style stuccoed buildings in the manner of those at London's Regent's Park, designed by John Nash. Tebbott succeeded in his venture and bequeathed the new No. 12 Park Street to his daughter, Sarah, who married

Above: Nos 12–16 Park Street, built by Robert Tebbott and completed in 1830.

Right: Fine Regency-style terraces imitating the great John Nash.

surgeon William Brown Holderness. Further residents included John Secker, who became a notable town clerk of Windsor, and Isaac Onslow, described as of Lincoln's Inn, 'magistrate of police'.

The buildings today retain their Regency style and their façades remain intact and are the only examples in Windsor of this style of architecture.

25. Baptist Chapel, Victoria Street, Windsor

How did other denominations in Windsor fare? Revd John Stoughton wrote in 1862 that the Victoria Street Chapel opened in 1832. The congregation had formerly assembled in a small Presbyterian church in the High Street, originally the theatre, which they took over when the new theatre was built on Thames Street. The Independent congregation is the oldest body of Dissenters in the town. It originated in the latter part of the eighteenth century, and, at first, being very small, occupied a building not far from the present one called 'the Hole in the Wall'. An inconvenient place of worship, it was afterwards fitted up in Bier Lane, where the good people were occasionally disturbed in divine service. The Wesleyan

The Baptist Chapel on Victoria Street.

The Baptist Chapel, opened in 1839.

denomination, at a much later period, built a small chapel in the same lane, on the opposite side, but removed in 1836 to the edifice in Peascod Street. The Baptist Chapel on Victoria Street was opened in 1839. It is an unusual example in Windsor of a neoclassical building. The stuccoed façade of this building is dominated by Ionic pilasters of its attached portico.

26. The Royal Mews, Windsor

The name 'mews' is a British name for a row or courtyard of stables and carriage houses with living quarters above them. The word mews comes from the Royal Mews, or royal stables, built 500 years ago on a former royal hawk mews. The Royal Mews in Windsor are situated on St Alban's Street, and houses a number of the queen's carriages and in particular the Ascot carriages, together with vehicles used in Windsor Great Park. Some horses for riding (rather than driving) are also stabled here. The relatively plain brick range with their large double doors was designed by architect Edward Blore. Although part of the castle, the mews are very much part of the townscape outside of the castle walls. At the end of the mews is Blore's castellated gatehouse to the Royal Riding School, completed with the mews in 1842. The name of the street is derived from Nell Gwyn's first son by Charles II, who was created Earl of St Albans.

The Royal Mews.

27. Holy Trinity Church, Trinity Place, Windsor

What was the centrepiece of a new middle-class development being developed by James Bedborough to the south-west of the old town? A new church. The foundation stone was laid by the Prince Consort in 1842 and the officers of the various regiments of guards contributed many of the interior fittings. Holy Trinity Church opened in 1844 and was built partly because of pressure from Prince Albert. Edward Blore was the architect and was well known, having been the architectural advisor to William IV and who was to finish the remodeling of Buckingham Palace in the late 1830s. Sir Watkin Williams Wynn presented the choir stalls in memory of his nephew, who drowned in Windsor Weir, while the chapel to the south side of the chancel was erected in 1884 by the 1st Life Guards as a memorial to deceased officers in the regiment and others. An organ was unveiled in 1886 by the king and a clock was added in the diamond jubilee year of Queen Victoria.

This brick church sits in its own square with surrounding avenues leading towards it with a spacious interior. Holy Trinity was to serve an affluent area of Windsor and in particular many officers associated with the nearby garrison.

Holy Trinity Church.

28. Windsor and Eton Central

29. Windsor and Eton Riverside

Windsor is served by two impressive railway stations: Windsor and Eton Central on the High Street and Windsor and Eton Riverside closer to the River Thames.

With the rapid expansion of the railways in the 1830s the Great Western Railway company constructed a line from London to Bristol. Its aim was to build the link via Windsor but strong local opposition meant that Windsor was bypassed altogether and the line went via Slough instead.

The major opposition was from the two main landowners Eton College and the Crown. Eton's headmaster at the time was sure the railways were 'evil', and that 'anything that brings Eton nearer to London is prejudicial to the school'. He also feared the effect of so many trains on his boys, stating 'I think the love of breaking windows is innate in all boys.' Edward Coleridge, senior assistant master, went further: 'any man would like to play cricket to bowl through an arch of 14 feet. I do not suppose that they would like to pitch the wicket one on each side of a viaduct 14 feet high'. The palace was even less keen. Prince Albert feared the vibrations would cause the castle to collapse and Queen Victoria was fearful of the pollution levels so close to the castle.

In the end, however, two lines were constructed. This was due not only to growing pressure from the public and the railway companies but also the Crown's need for money to fund its ambitious redevelopment schemes. The castle reconstruction costs had caused a public outcry so the offer of £60,000 from London & Southwestern and £25,000 from Great Western ensured the railways' eventual arrival. The Crown had hoped for just one line but the intense competition between the two companies made this impossible. Both pledged to build stations that would provide accommodation for the personal use, privacy and comfort of the monarch and their entourages and safeguards were set in place to protect the Eton boys. This also set up a race to see who would get to Windsor first. After many setbacks and accidents, Great Western opened their line first in October 1849 and South Western opened in December of the same year.

The Crown were able to fund the widening and improvement of Thames Street and the High Street, new roads to both Old Windsor and Datchet, as well as two new bridges, Victoria Bridge and Albert Bridge, and new drains for the castle and town.

Windsor and Eton Central Railway Station

Originally called Windsor and renamed Windsor and Eton Central in 1949 following the nationalisation of the railways, the station is approached by an impressive brick viaduct and a wrought-iron bridge designed by Isambard Kingdom Brunel and is

Central railway station, now pedestrianised and a popular retail centre. (http://exploretheworld.co.nz/windsor.html)

Above: Central railway station was rebuilt in 1897.

Below: Central railway station and its glazed girder roof.

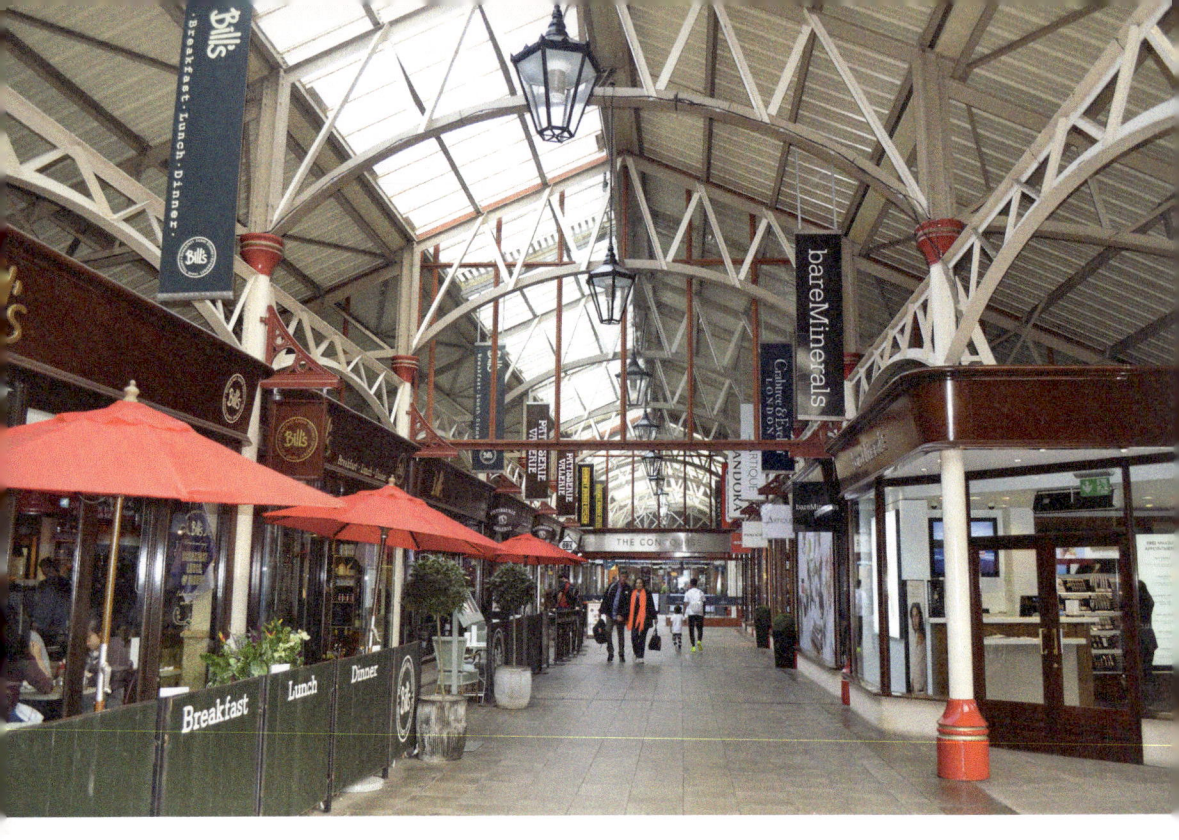

Central railway station, now popular retail outlets.

a bowstring construction with a single span of 202 feet between brick abutments. It was finished in 1849. The original station building had to be much improved for increasing demand and was rebuilt in 1897 to commemorate Queen Victoria's Jubilee at a cost of nearly £50,000 on the site of the infamous George Street slum. It had four platforms and sidings and included the imposing pedimented Dutch gable archway over the entrance from the High Street (now pedestrianised). It had booking halls for first-, second- and third-class passengers and separate waiting rooms for each. A magnificent glazed girder roof was constructed over luxurious royal rooms, built to accommodate parties from the castle.

With the decline of the railways, the station lost three of its four platforms and retained just one truncated line providing a service to Slough. Today the building is called Windsor Royal Shopping and consists of shops, restaurants and coffee shops. However, the character of the station is still most evident and provides a real feeling for what the station must have been like in its heyday.

Windsor and Eton Riverside Station

Constructed by Sir William Tite and completed in 1851 of a brick Tudor Gothic design with mullioned and transomed windows, gables and multi-arched entrance, the Riverside station is a Grade II listed building. It too catered for Queen Victoria with an ornate reception room and even a look out turret from which any royal arrival could be observed and staff forewarned. The station has a wrought-iron canopy roof with tall arched doors along one side, not only to allow travellers

Above: Windsor & Eton Riverside, completed in 1851.

Right: Windsor & Eton Riverside, which once catered for Queen Victoria.

to walk directly from the train to their awaiting carriages but also designed to allow the household cavalry easy access without dismounting. Today the station continues to connect Windsor with London Waterloo.

30. Queen's Terrace, King's Road, Windsor

One of the more important architectural developments of the eighteenth century was the high-class terrace, derived from those fashionable places such as Bath and Edinburgh. This particular innovation came at a late stage to Windsor as there was

Above: Queen's Terrace, designed by Samuel Teulon in 1849.

Left: Built in the Jacobean style, with ornate gables.

no requirement for it in a period when the town suffered from the neglect of the castle. After George III's return, a small number of terraces were built, particularly in the early nineteenth century and along King's Road, close to the Home Park. In design, these stock-brick rows were very similar to contemporary work in London and the fashionable bathing resorts of Brighton and Margate. Eventually going down-market elsewhere, in Windsor the grand terrace did survive into the mid-Victorian era and none more so than at Queen's Terrace.

Samuel Teulon's eccentric Queen's Terrace in King's Road is a deliberate attempt by the architect at historicism, bringing to life the idea of the great Jacobean mansions of the early seventeenth century. Built in 1849, it is a barely restrained 'riot of brick and stone, prickling with chimneys and shaped gables'.

31. Windsor Barracks (Victoria and Combermere)

Windsor has been a garrison town since the Civil War. Victoria Barracks were built in Windsor in 1853 and were later enlarged in 1911. These old barracks were eventually demolished in 1988 with the new barracks constructed between 1989 and 1993. These barracks have played an important part in the life of Windsor and they remain the location from where troops set off from to change the guard at Windsor Castle. The Coldstream Guards, who have been based at the barracks since 2011, will remain here until 2019.

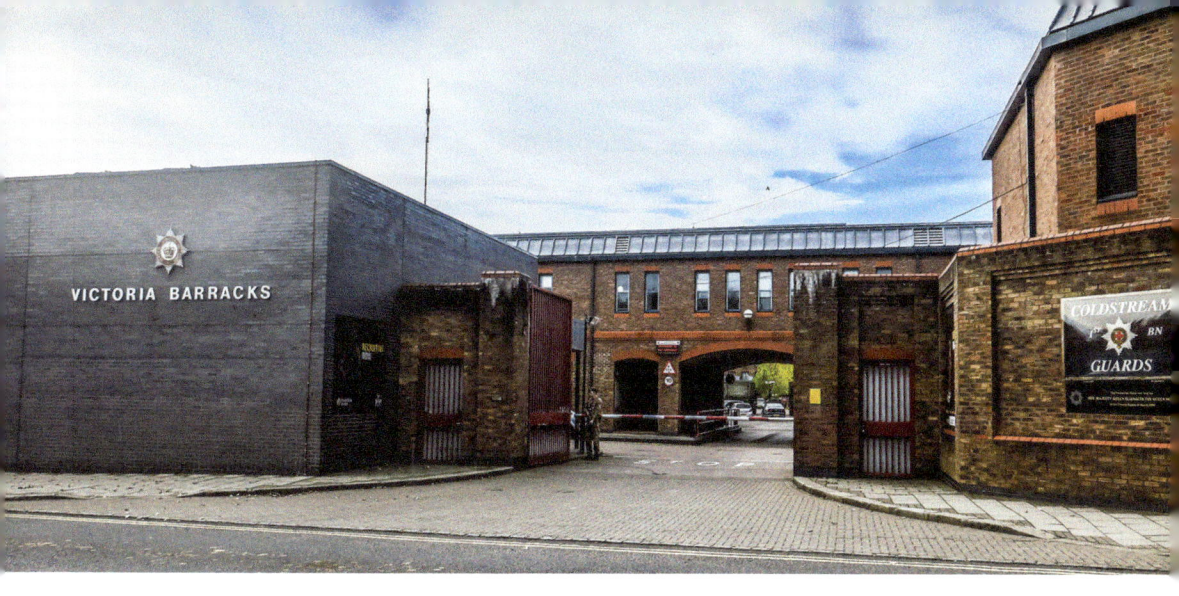

Victoria Barracks.

The other barracks in Windsor are equally important to the town. Known originally as Clewer Barracks, they were designed to accommodate the Royal Horse Guards and were built at Clewer Park between 1796 and 1800. It was Queen Victoria who ordered the replacement of these barracks after she visited in 1864 and, as a result, it exposed to her the barracks' unhygienic conditions. The eventual new barracks were named after Field Marshal Lord Combermere and included a riding school, which was built in 1881. The barracks were improved further in 2006 and became the home of the Household Cavalry Regiment. By 2019, though, the regiment moved to Warminster with only No. 18 Troop and the training wing remaining. Further changes included the addition of the 1st Battalion, Welsh Guards, who will be moving in to start their ceremonial duties in Windsor.

32. Eton Porny School, No. 29 High Street, Eton

Antoine Pyron du Martre is best known by his adopted name of Mark Anthony Porny, who was born at Caen in Normandy and came from France in 1754 at the age of twenty-three. After considerable struggles to maintain himself, he eventually settled down as French Master in Eton in 1773, and occupied this position for thirty-three years.

In 1790, attempts were being made by Provost Roberts to establish a charity and Sunday school for the children of the parish. A committee of twenty-two was appointed and subscriptions were collected, which enabled the fine work to be carried on in a small way from year to year. This was the first attempt, since the college was founded, to give the children of the poor a religious and elementary education, and it was Mark Anthony Porny who became very interested in these endeavours.

With his teaching and writing of school books, Porny saved approximately £4,000 and on his death, it was discovered that 'in gratitude for the little property he had

Above: A dedication to Mark Antony Porny.

Left: The former Eton Porny School, dedicated to Mark Antony Porny, opened in 1813.

Below: The later Porny School, built to the designs of G. E. Street.

The Eton Porny School today, built in High Victorian Gothic style.

acquired in this free and generous kingdom he had bequeathed the bulk of it upon trust unto the Treasurer of the Charity and Sunday School established in Eton in the County of Bucks, to be applied by the Trustees or Committee or by whatsoever name they may be designated for the time being, towards carrying out the laudable and useful designs of its institution'. Mr Charles Knight, printer and bookseller of New Windsor, was appointed Porny's executor. Unfortunately, there were delays in carrying out his bequest, as a result of a lawsuit instituted by some distant French relatives. The money gained in interest had become worth £8,250 by the time the plaintiffs were defeated in their attempt to upset the will, and in 1813 steps were taken to build a master and mistress's house, now known as Nos 129A and B High Street, with two schoolrooms behind that now serve as the Parish Room. Buildings were constructed by Mr Tebbott of Windsor at a cost of £1,723 and were described as 'neat and convenient buildings, in conformity with plans submitted to the Court of Chancery'. The school was opened on 26 April 1813, the management of it being vested in the Provost and Fellows and eight other inhabitants of the parish, who were called Porny Trustees. After paying for the cost of building, there still remained an endowment of £5,200, the interest of which enabled the Porny Trustees to give a free education to ninety children. According to the old rules these scholars were elected from the Sunday schools, being the children of parishioners of Eton, born in wedlock, having been not less than one year in the Sunday school, and regular and punctual in their attendance. The Porny Trustees used to meet on the first Tuesday in each month except during the holidays. Every Porny scholar who reached the age of fourteen, and left school with a good character, received a bible and prayer book.

By the middle of the nineteenth century, the school and master's house were built further down the High Street to the designs of G. E. Street in High Victorian

Gothic style with the original schoolroom extended in 1873 by the addition of a large two-storey range.

Porny's work was recognised, when he was appointed by George III, one of the Poor Knights of Windsor, and on his death in 1802 was buried on the south side of St George's Chapel, where his grave is still to be seen with its Latin inscription.

33. Prince Consort Cottages, Windsor

The Prince Consort Cottages were completed in 1855 to the designs of architect Henry Roberts for the Royal Windsor Society in close consultation with Prince Albert. The Prince Consort was the High Steward of the Borough from 1850, and was wholly engrossed in the hopes and aspirations for the future betterment of the town. He personally oversaw the design and building of these small but simple gabled red-brick cottages ranged around a green. These houses were effective accommodation for his workers on the farms and he also oversaw the creation of a new farm inside the Home Park, and the overhaul of two other farms in the Great Park, which he would go on to manage as a successful business venture until his death in 1861.

Prince Consort Cottages.

34. Almshouses, Victoria Street, Windsor

Along Victoria Street by Batchelor's Acre you can find the very distinctive Windsor almshouses. They were opened by Queen Victoria in 1863. In a time of changing attitudes to the poor, these almshouses were for worthy working-class pensioners and at the time cost £3,500. They were restored in 1989 and reopened by the Queen Mother as Ellison House, after the Victorian vicar of Windsor, Canon Ellison. Surrounding a courtyard in a 'u' form in a strong high Gothic Revival ecclesiastical style, they are constructed of red and yellow brickwork, stone dressings and steep slate roofs with timber-framed spirelets. Built in the same year close by in Chariott's Place, you can find Chariott's Charity, an almshouse built in a very similar style, again with steep pitched roofs and a central spirelet. Chariott's charity is a very distinctive building financed by Joseph Chariott. A member of the Congregational

Chariott's Charity almshouse in Gothic Revival style.

Above: Ellison House almshouses, opened in 1863.

Below left: Ellison House, reopened in 1989 by Queen Elizabeth, the Queen Mother.

Below right: Gothic Revival details to Ellison House.

Above left: An intriguing shield on Ellison House.

Above right: Detail on Ellison House.

church, Joseph Chariott made his fortune as a local builder and property developer. On his death in 1848 at the age of ninety-one he left all his money to the church and charities. It is reported his fortune was found in pickle jars in cash at his home and had to be taken to the bank in a cart of which the bottom fell out.

35. Peascod Street, Windsor

Peascod Street is possibly one of the oldest streets in Windsor. The road itself follows what is a natural watershed and from the earliest of times it was a routeway between forest, castle and a river crossing via the Datchet ferry to Colnbrook and then on towards London. There have been a number of variations of the name of the street including Puscroftstrate and Pescrofstrate from the thirteenth century. The first mention of Pesecod is in a lease of 1335. In the fourteenth and fifteenth centuries, Pesecod and Puscod were almost interchangeable. The name Peascod itself is derived from the croft where peas were grown. Peas and beans were an important part of the medieval diet.

By 1607 houses existed on both sides of Peascod Street and there are references in 1635 to 'paving a good part of the gutter in Peascod Street'. Richard Topham, Windsor's MP from 1698 to 1713, lived in Peascod Street in the early part of the eighteenth century when it remained primarily residential. Topham was also Keeper of the Tower of London, a man of erudition and taste and a large local landowner. His house, Pilgrim Place, was on the south side of Peascod Street and was reputed to have been adorned with marble fountains and a fine collection of statues, pictures and medals.

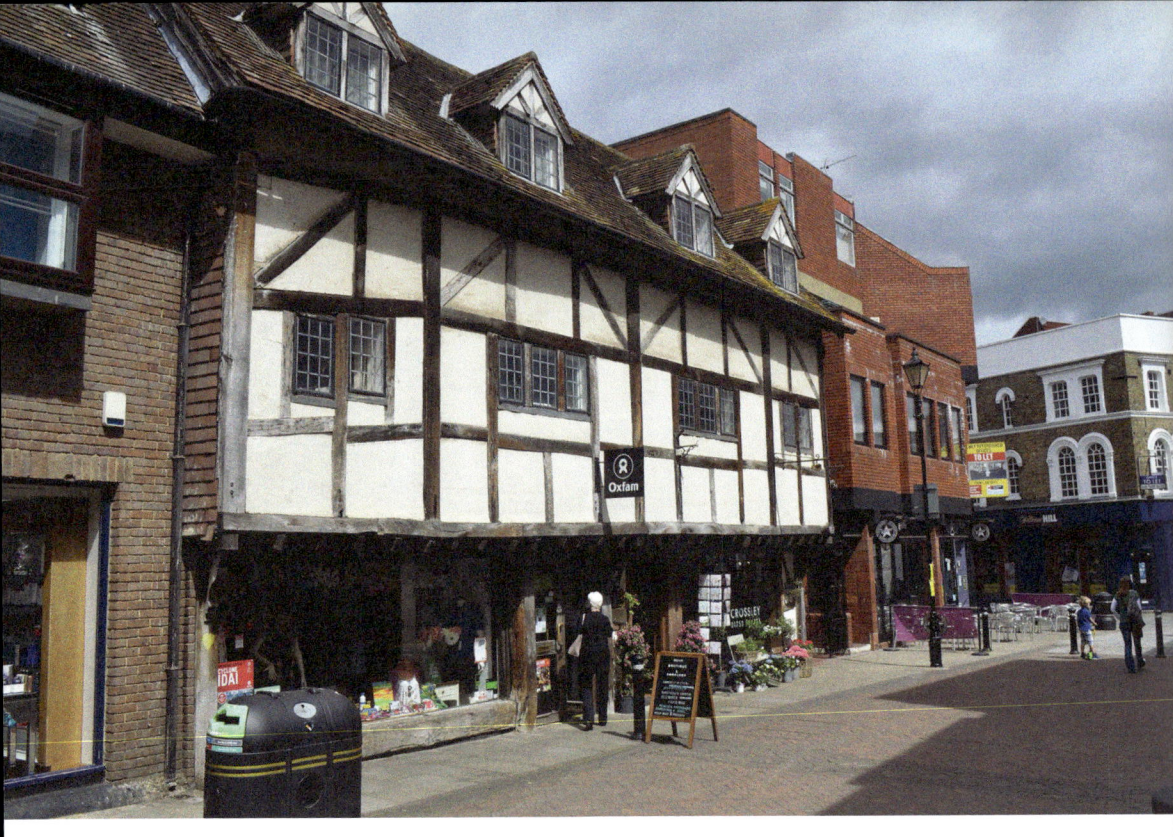

Above: Nos 86–87 Peascod Street is claimed to date from the fifteenth century but is probably *c.* 1600. It was restored in 1976.

Below: No. 91 Peascod Street, a nineteenth-century, three-storey yellow-brick corner building with distinctive painted stone windows and bold rendered parapet.

Above: Looking up Peascod Street to the castle.

Below: This Gothic building in Peascod Street has a hint of Venetian and dates from 1866.

Above: The current Barclays Bank on the corner of Peascod Street and the High Street. It is a classically styled, late nineteenth-century, three-storey, attic ashlar stone corner building.

Below: One of Windsor's most celebrated stores is W. J. Daniel of Windsor and has been in existence since 1901. It was recently modernised for the twenty-first century.

Peascod Street has managed to retain some characteristics of its medieval history through the continuation of long thin burgage plots (tenure by which land or property in a town was held in return for service or annual rent) and some medieval buildings that still remain. A further medieval feature that has remained is the presence of long thin alleyways leading through ground-floor openings between retail units and large open backlands beyond. It certainly appears much of the medieval fabric of Peascod Street survived up until the twentieth century. However, from this time plots were amalgamated to accommodate modern retail needs as the street moved from residential to its current use. These modern developments have had mixed results with preservation, restoration and introductions all prevalent – not all introductions so sympathetic to the streetscape. The demolition of the streets to the north-west of Peascod Street has allowed large-scale retail units to develop, which has helped to maintain, to some extent, the original grain of Peascod Street. The King Edward Court development was originally designed in the 1970s and was extended and redeveloped in 2007. This is an example of successful modern integration in a historic retail area.

One of the more interesting buildings has sadly disappeared. At No. 133 is the site of the Star & Garter public house. A pub since 1719, the Star & Garter was also famous as a boxing gym used by many fighters often preparing for title fights, most famously Sugar Ray Robinson in 1951. In 1962, the upstairs rooms became infamous as the Ricky Tick rhythm and blues club, hosting such famous names as The Yardbirds, The Who, Bill Haley and even the Rolling Stones until the venue was switched to bigger premises in Clewer Mead in 1965. Today the original building no longer exists, replaced by a modern retail unit.

36. All Saints Church, Windsor

It was Revd Ellison, the vicar of Windsor, who became aware, when the chancel was added to St John's, of the lack of pew spaces available for the less well-off in the expanding town. Ellison began a fund to which Queen Victoria was to donate £300 to finance a new church for the town: what was to become All Saints Church in Frances Road. It was the Queen's favourite daughter, Victoria, the Princess Royal, who had become Crown princess of Prussia in 1858, who laid the foundation stone of this new church in 1863 while visiting home. The church was designed by architect Arthur Blomfield and was described as High Victorian Gothic, built of red brick with bold bands of blue on the outside.

Often considered quite plain, its main ornamental feature is the large, plate-traceried round window at the west end, and a spirelet-topped belfry above the east end of the nave. Another well-known anecdote is that the poet and novelist Thomas Hardy was allegedly involved in the design of the church as he was working nearby at the time.

All Saints Church. (© Bill Boaden)

37. Church of St Edward the Confessor, Windsor

The name of St Edward the Confessor has long been associated with Windsor. He was a favourite saint of both Henry II and Henry III, and soon after his canonisation, a chapel dedicated to him was built within the walls of Windsor Castle. The chapel is now known as the Albert Memorial Chapel.

The parish was founded in 1825, and until the present church was built, the parishioners were served by a small chapel in Hermitage Road. The first parish priest was P. A. Comberbach (1825–30), followed by T. F. Wilkinson (1830–54). The third parish priest was Augustus Applegard, who served the community for thirty-five years and was responsible for building the church in 1868. He was followed by John Loginotto, who was parish priest for over forty-seven years from 1889 until 1936.

The church was designed by little-known architect Charles Alban Buckler and was opened on St Edward's Day, 13 October 1868, in the presence of Archbishop, later Cardinal, Henry Edward Manning. Buckler built a Gothic Revival church of rough ragstone, which cost in the region of £4,000. Although it has no tower, but a tall clerestorey, it is a striking building. In 2005, St Edward's Church was voted Windsor's favourite listed building.

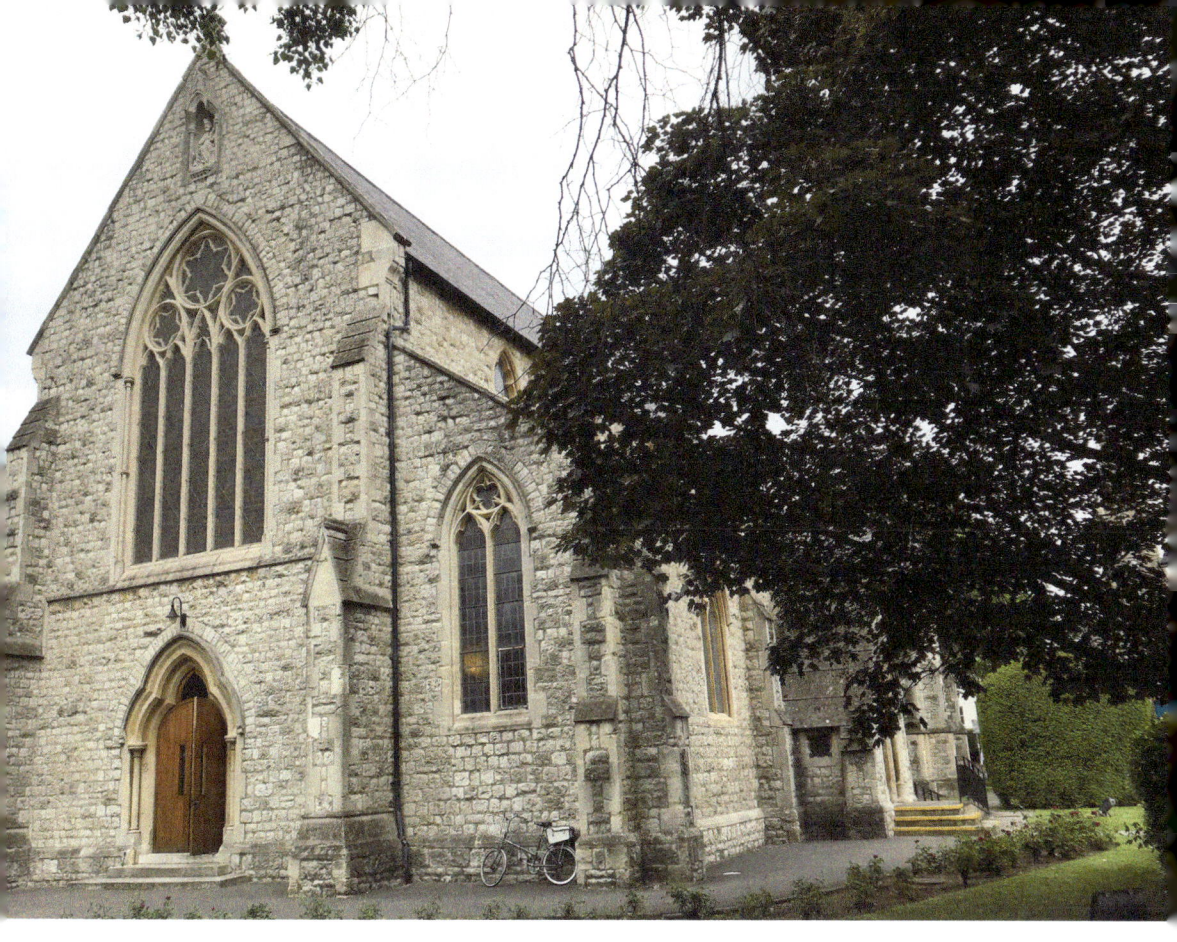

Church of St Edward the Confessor.

38. The Templars Hall, St Leonard's Road, Windsor

There has been some local debate on the impressive building on St Leonard's Road, known as the Templars Hall. The building dates from 1874 and was referred to in *The Times* of 24 March 1890 in the context of 'WINDSOR–The contest for the representation of Windsor opened on Saturday, when Mr. W. H. Grenfell, the Liberal candidate, who had previously begun canvassing, was formally introduced by Mr. T. D. Bolton M.P. to the burgesses at the Good Templars Hall in the evening...'

The Templars Hall was, in fact, the meeting place of the Order of the Good Templars and was mostly used for public meetings, which ranged from meetings of the Liberals to a lecture given by the great social reformer and women's rights campaigner Annie Besant in 1890. The International Organisation of Good Templars was founded in 1851 as the Independent Order of Good Templars (IOGT), and is a fraternal organisation describing itself as 'the premier global interlocutor for evidence-based policy measures and community-based interventions to prevent and reduce harm caused by alcohol and other drugs'. It also claims to be the largest worldwide community of non-governmental

The Templars Hall.

organisations with a mission to independently enlighten people around the world on a lifestyle free from alcohol and other drugs.

Today, the IOGT is a leading non-governmental organisation in the temperance movement. Its headquarters of IOGT International are situated in Stockholm, Sweden. The IOGT named themselves after the Knights Templar, citing the legend that the original knights 'drank sour milk, and also because they were fighting a great crusade against this terrible vice of alcohol.'

39. Harte & Garter Hotel, High Street, Windsor

One of the most historic hotels in Windsor is the Harte & Garter, which is an amalgamation of two fourteenth-century inns: The Garter Inn, named after the Most Noble Order of the Garter, which was founded by Edward III; and The White Harte, named in honour of the royal emblem worn by Richard II. In the late nineteenth century, they were joined together to form the Harte & Garter Hotel – the building we see today.

The 50 Buildings

There is a brief mention of the earliest alehouses in the records held by Windsor Corporation in 1528 whereby rentals were shown as payable for a number of establishments. There were over twenty establishments mentioned at the time including The Mermaid, The Black Eagle, The Goat, The Maidenhead, The White Harte and The White Lion. It is worth noting that Windsor Corporation appeared to be the owners of a least fifteen of them. About this time, the royal court was often at Windsor and the demand was growing for new inns and alehouses to satisfy the town's increasing number of visitors. Windsor Corporation were not slow in leasing some of their properties to meet this trend. St George's Chapel saw the way things were going and surviving property deeds show that in Tudor times they owned The Angel, The Broad Arrow, The Bull by Windsor Bridge as well as The Crown, The Hartshorn, The Swan, The Talbot and The White Horse. Four of these were inns.

In a catalogue of 1636 compiled by John Taylor, a waterman of London, The Cross Keys, The Garter, The George and The White Hart were listed as taverns. Others were classified as either inns or alehouses. The 1552 Licensing Act marked the beginning of a period of increasing restrictions on the sale of ale and beer. Parliament, Council Chambers and pulpits condemned alehouses as the meeting places of people of disrepute, 'nests of Satan' and the focus of public disorder. Accordingly, licensees were required to enter into bonds, or recognisances, that they would not allow disorderly behaviour or harbour rogues and vagabonds. In the reign of James I (1603–25) further laws were introduced to 'restrain the

An early view of the White Harte.

The Harte & Garter Hotel. (© Paul the Archivist, CC BY-SA 4.0)

inordinate tippling in inns, alehouses and other victualling houses', and to prevent the 'loathsome and odious sin of drunkenness'. Failure to obey led to a period of time spent in the stocks. Windsor was a Puritan town and the stocks stood almost opposite The Mermaid Inn. Records kept for the year 1618 indicate thirty-four men – both innkeepers and lehouse keepers – appeared before the town magistrates for breaking these laws.

Thankfully today, the use of the stocks is no more and the Harte & Garter is one of the town's most popular hotels.

40. No. 10 Alma Road, Windsor

The block of six modest Victorian terraced houses at the bottom of Alma Road are significant because at No. 10 you can find the birthplace of Sir Sydney Camm CBE FRAeS, the designer of the Second World War single-seater fighter aircraft the Hawker Hurricane. He was born here on 5 August 1893. Sir Sydney was the eldest child of twelve siblings. His younger brother Fred Camm became a technical author and editor well known for the *Practical* series of magazines.

The 50 Buildings

Sir Sydney attended the Royal Free School on Bachelor's Acre and at the age of fifteen, following in his father's footsteps, became an apprentice carpenter. At this time, he and his brother gained a reputation for building model aircraft, which they sold to Herbert's on Eton High Street, allegedly illicitly to the boys at Eton School. As a founder of the Windsor Model Aircraft and Gliding Club, he helped build a man-carrying glider which was flown in Windsor Home Park in 1913 (just a decade after the Wright brothers). The site of their workshop was located close to their home on Alma Road opposite Arthur Road where today the Ward Royal estate now stands.

In 1914 Sir Sydney worked for the Martinsyde Aircraft Company at Brooklands as a shop floor carpenter and was quickly promoted to draughtsman in the design office. He joined the Hawker Aircraft Company in 1923 as a senior draughtsman. Sir Sydney was responsible for the creation of fifty-two different aircraft of which 26,000 were manufactured from the Cygnet biplane in 1924 to the Vertical Take Off and Landing P1127 in 1960, the development aircraft that led to the Hawker Siddeley Harrier. The Hawker Hurricane is probably the most famous due to its contribution during the Second World War. An aircraft that was easy to fly and easy to maintain yet still fast agile and strong, it was very popular with aircrew and ground crew alike. Sir Sydney Camm died in Richmond on 12 March 1966. Close by at the end of Barry Avenue behind Alexandra Gardens stands a full-size replica of Hawker Hurricane as a memorial to one of the most prolific aircraft designers of all time.

Above: No. 10 Alma Road.

Right: In memory of Sir Sydney Camm (1893–1966).

41. High Street (various), Eton

Over time Eton has evolved into a linear pattern along the main street leading up and away from the river until it reaches the college, where the street pattern changes to an open one with wider roads that branch off and terminate in a gradual curve towards Datchet and Slough. The High Street curves gently to align with Windsor Castle and the bridge to the south and the college to the north. It has a delightful compact shape, with open lammas land to the west, and the river bounding the south and east sides. There is a network of narrower, primarily residential, streets and connecting paths leading off the lower part of the High Street.

The development of Eton has been primarily influenced by the location of two major uses, Windsor Castle and Eton College, and it is these institutions that still dominate Eton today. The northern end of the High Street is dominated by the college buildings and their associated uses while it is the southern end of the town that holds the majority of the commercial element of Eton. Today, however, the tourist who visits the castle also often visits Eton, and so many of the shops have uses such as galleries, antique shops and gift shops and there are now a significant number of restaurants and public houses. There is also an unusual mix of shops and services for the college. These include barbers and outfitters, stationers and the services such as laundry and catering.

Within the High Street are a number of non-listed buildings which were originally built for specific functions, some of which are now redundant. The former National Westminster Bank building has some good quality brickwork with very fine mortar joints, and a richly moulded terracotta frieze, and is dated 1894. Next door to this is Barclays Bank, which has a handsome façade of red brick and carved stone from 1931. The old police station at No. 54 is a prominent red-brick, art deco-style building.

An early postcard view of Eton High Street.

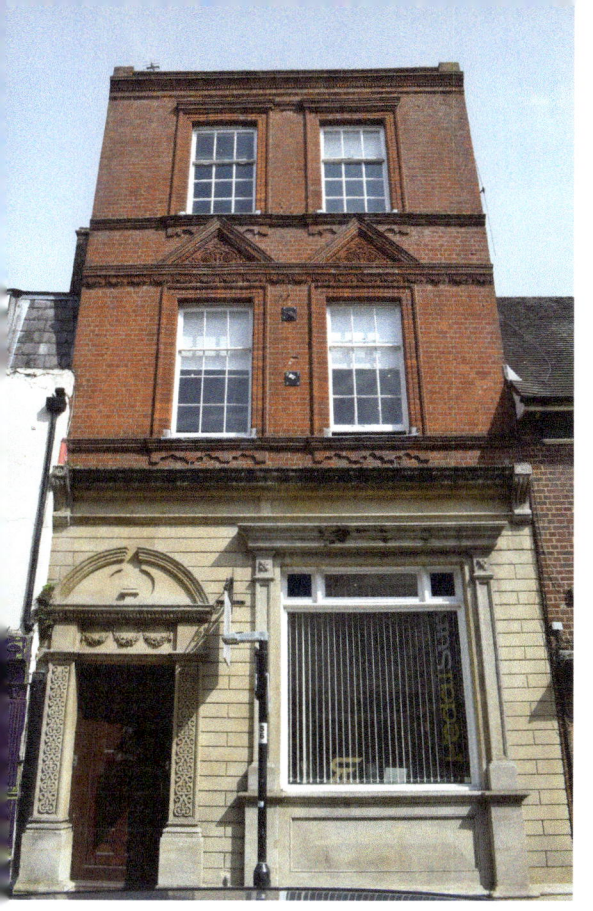

Above left: No. 54, a former police station, is art deco in style.

Above right: The entrance to No. 54 High Street.

Right: Former National Westminster Bank, dated 1894.

Above: Barclays Bank, Eton High Street.

Below: No. 17 High Street, Eton.

42. Former Queensmead School, Windsor

The elegant Victorian mansion that houses the former Queensmead School in Windsor was designed by Scottish architect W. F. Lyon, FRIBA, for Henri C. J. Henry of the Old Windsor Tapestry Manufactory, who leased the land from the Crown Commissioners in 1880.

The late Victorian period was a time when old craft skills using hand and eye rather than machines were being revived, notably by the artist William Morris. Tapestry weaving, considered by Morris to be the finest form of textile craft, was one of them, and he established his own tapestry works in 1881. However, Morris was pre-empted by a firm based in nearby Old Windsor. The Old Windsor Tapestry Manufactory was founded in 1876 by two Frenchmen: Marcel Brignolas, as manager, and Henri C. J. Henry as its first director. Henry was art director of Gillows, Oxford Street, London. They brought weavers over from the famous French Aubusson works, and set up their looms in Manor Lodge in Straight Road, Old Windsor, a building since demolished. The 1881 census shows a large number of families from Aubusson or Paris living in the village. Wives worked as tapestry repairers and children received some education at a school held at the Lord Nelson public house where the wool dyeing works were first set up.

The Old Windsor Tapestry Manufactory was one of only two tapestry works to be established in England in the nineteenth century, the other being that of William Morris at Merton Abbey. The Old Windsor Tapestry Manufactory enjoyed royal

The former Queensmead School. Its future use is in doubt after the school closed in 2019.

patronage as Prince Leopold, Duke of Albany, the youngest son of Queen Victoria, enthusiastically supported the project, becoming its president. The Royal Windsor Tapestry Works are known for some very detailed and magnificent designs during their short lifetime. These include the famous Merry Wives of Windsor, a series of eight award-winning panels that won gold medal in Paris in 1878.

As the Royal Windsor Tapestry Works grew in popularity Queen Victoria took an interest in the designs and encouraged other royals to commission pieces. Another famous design emerging from Royal Windsor and commissioned by the Marchioness of Lorne was a tapestry celebrating *Much Ado About Nothing*. It is thought that this is the piece that now hangs in Buckingham Palace. The Queen's Sofa, which has two cartoons of detailed and delicate wild roses worked into the design and Queen Victoria's monogram, is a well-known Royal Windsor piece and is now part of the Royal Collection.

The sudden death of Prince Leopold in 1884 spelled out demise for Royal Windsor and the factory began to decline after a short life producing highly detailed and unique designs. Rather than associate royalty with a bankrupt factory the decision was taken to close the works in 1890. Many of the French workers, including the Foussadier family, left England for America, taking the Aubusson way of working into an emerging new market and developing their expertise in the New World.

Henry's former mansion was to change hands and it was the Brigidine Sisters who established a convent and school here in 1948, the second such founded by the order in England and Wales. The Victorian bricked mansion built for Henry that the Sisters moved into remained one of the school's main buildings. The school was later run by lay staff but retained its Catholic ethos and religious character. During the early 2000s, the school experienced financial difficulties; pupil and staff numbers declined and the school was threatened with closure. In 2012, further funding was secured and the school remained open and independent and in 2018 it was renamed from Brigidine to Queensmead. It finally closed in 2019.

43. Nos 67–69 Victoria Street

It was incredibly popular during Queen Victoria's reign that royal street naming became commonplace and this was present in Windsor too. The 'New Road' created in 1823 to go from Sheet Street to Dedworth was renamed Victoria Street, Clarence Road and Dedworth Road by the 1850s.

A number of fine buildings are found on Victoria Street and include houses, public houses and places of worship. Dated 1888 is the High Victorian Gothic building at No. 67. Two storeys high and built with stock brick with a stuccoed ground floor, it consists of a carriage way and double shop front with pointed arches, pitched granite columns with foliate capitals, and pointed fanlights. The building has been altered but the 'over the top' decoration was clearly making an architectural statement with its passageway leading to a rear yard with workshops. Next door is an early nineteenth-century two-storey stucco fronted building with

Nos 67–69 Victoria Street are highly embellished.

parapet coping, recently a restaurant. The building was a mid-nineteenth-century shopfront and possibly residential at some stage.

The use of stucco was prevalent in Windsor and was a render lined to resemble stone, but later often painted and was much in vogue in the early nineteenth century.

44. The Old Court and Former Fire Station, Windsor

The foundation stone for this fine Edwardian building was laid in 1905 by Sir William Shipley and in 1907 it opened as Windsor's magistrates' court, police station and fire station. The building remains very similar to this day, although the magistrates' court, police station and fire station have all since been relocated.

The Old Court is now a vibrant arts and entertainment centre with a screen cinema sitting in the Old Court, the first time digital cinema has ever been available in Windsor.

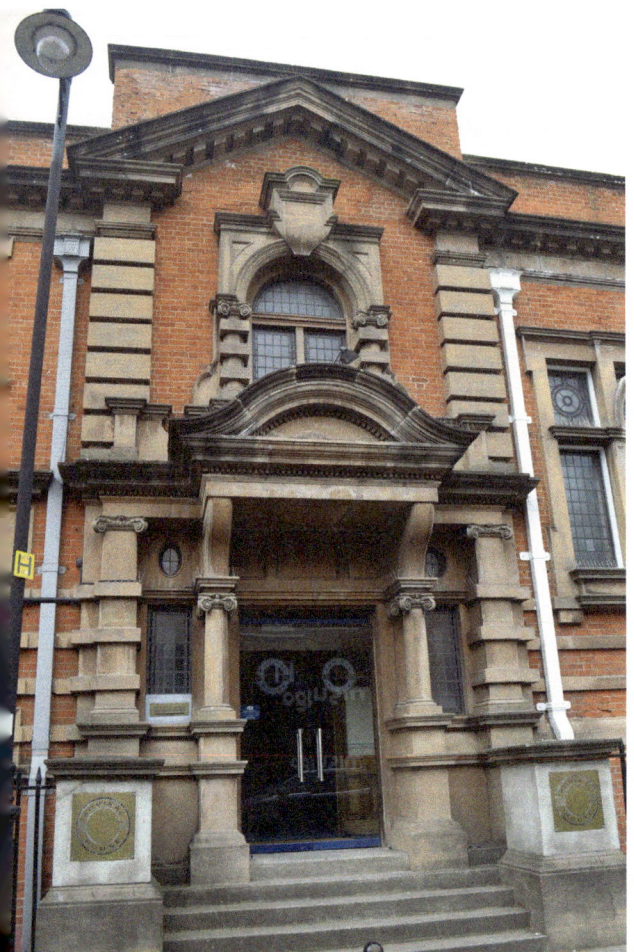

Above: Former fire station and courthouse.

Left: A grand entrance to the old courthouse.

45. King Edward VII Hospital, Windsor

With a rapidly growing population in Windsor at the end of the nineteenth century, the provision of the Windsor Dispensary in Church Street and the old infirmary at Batchelor's Acre were proving critically inadequate for the growing demand. The mayor, William Shipley, set up a fund that raised £13,000 to construct a new medical facility. The site was identified opposite Combermere Barracks as a location suitable for a new hospital, away from the town centre on St Leonard's Road, and was apparently near the site of St Peter's Leper Hospital, founded in 1168. The building was designed by A. W. West, in Queen Anne revival style. The commemoration stone of Siberian marble was laid by Edward VII on 22 June 1908 and the building was officially opened on 17 March 1909. It had fifty beds in two wards: on the west side the King Edward ward for men and the Queen Alexandra ward for women. The eastern ward was the Helena children's ward and the ground floor was the Barry ward for accident and emergencies. They had a modern light and roomy operating theatre with modern equipment and a horse-drawn ambulance service.

In 1916, the hospital was used for the treatment of casualties from the front line in France, receiving its first injured men on 22 September 1916 directly from the Somme battlefield. The hospital quickly became specialised in the treatment of

King Edward VII Hospital, built in Queen Anne revival style.

King Edward VII Hospital.

combat injuries. On 3 May 1918 an orthopedic treatment room was established specifically for the treatment of disabled soldiers.

On Tuesday 24 April 1928, a defective flue above the Queen Alexandra ward started a fire in an inaccessible area, destroying the western wing of the hospital. Fortunately, the fire was extinguished in fifteen minutes due to the actions of the fire brigade and troops from the barracks opposite, who were able to evacuate the wards and salvage furniture, bedding and equipment. There were no casualties and the military hospital facilities were able to accommodate the patients. Today the hospital no longer has wards but accommodates clinics serving the local area.

46. Theatre Royal, Windsor

In the shadow of the castle at the bottom of Thames Street sits the Theatre Royal, Windsor, in a beautiful Edwardian building. Today it is the only unsubsidised producing theatre to operate all-year round, offering a wide range of productions from the classics, traditional pantomime to first productions.

There has been a Theatre Royal in Windsor since the eighteenth century. The first was little more than a shed in a muddy field in Peascod Street. In 1793, a larger more elegant building was constructed in the High Street, which was regularly attended by George III and Queen Charlotte. This building was sold to a religious group who promptly closed the theatre and converted it into a chapel. The local theatregoers were so distressed they raised £6,000 to build a new theatre in 1815 on the current theatre's site. Tragically this building burnt to the ground in 1908, making way for the construction of the present theatre in 1910.

The Theatre Royal was built for Sir William Shipley and Captain Reginald Shipley by J. Allen & Sons and designed by Frank Verity in early English Renaissance style. The theatre contains an auditorium of 850 seats and was designed to contain an asbestos fire curtain, which accounted for the buildings tall narrow façade, attracting complaints at the time as it upset some local resident's riverside views of the castle.

Theatre Royal on Thames Street.

The theatre experienced early mixed fortunes, briefly converting to a cinema in the 1930s, but the attendance of George VI and Queen Elizabeth to a production of *A Rose Without a Thorn* set a precedent of royal patronage that is continued today and cemented the theatres successful future. The theatre is a Grade II listed building with interiors designed by Carl Toms in 1965, which were refurbished in 1973 and 1994. Today Bill Kenwright is the theatre's executive producer and often the first productions shown here transfer to London's West End.

47. The Church of Our Lady of Sorrows, Eton

Built in 1914 and opened in January 1915, the Church of Our Lady of Sorrows in Eton was intended to serve as a place of worship for the Catholic Etonians and the townsfolk of Eton and Datchet. It was given to the town by Alfred, 5th Lord Braye (1849–1928).

At the time there was still considerable opposition to the Catholic Church. Lord Braye bought the piece of land originally for the purpose of building a 'bungalow' but when the Eton College authorities discovered the bungalow was to be a Catholic church, they did all in their power to prevent and stop the building work altogether. They invoked an ancient law regarding windows and another old law that prevented rainwater draining into surrounding land. As a result, all the windows are in the roof of the building and the gutters drain into a well at the

The Church of Our Lady of Sorrows, off Eton High Street.

back of the altar. Finally, after the church was opened they forbade the Catholic boys of the college to use it, and it was not until 1920 that the college boys were allowed to hear Mass in the church.

The building is of an unusual design, was built by Italian workmen and is based on a design of a Venetian chapel. It has fourteen different kinds of marble in its interior including black marble, which was left over from the building of the Royal Mausoleum. The care of the church was also given over to the Canons Regular of the Lateran, which is of historic interest since it was these canons who held the advowson of Eton in the thirteenth century.

48. Ward Royal, Windsor

Windsor's population trebled during the twentieth century and Ward Royal was built in response to the demand for housing close to the town centre. A large area of terraced housing was identified for demolition around the area bound by Arthur Road to the north, Alma Road to the west and Charles Street to the east. The new development cut Oxford Road in two, leaving Oxford Road as we know it today to the west and a short section, Oxford Road East, still joining Peascod Street.

Elizabeth II opened the development on 23 June 1969. It is very typical of housing developments at that time. Constructed of grey concrete, a complex of

The controversial Ward Royal estate, opened in 1969.

flats joined by ramps and staircases, it is not to everybody's taste and remains controversial. However, at the time it won prizes from the Ministry of Housing and Local Government and still provides spacious homes for a thriving community in walking distance of Windsor town centre.

49. Windsor Central, Windsor

One of Windsor's newest buildings is the rather fine office block called Windsor Dials, which houses a number of international companies. The name is unusual and the site was possibly once a brewery and was originally very run down and unpopular with local people. Windsor Central is also the home of the large Travelodge. With the continued growth of the town and its popularity with visitors and workers alike, Windsor has had to adapt from a small market town into a major shopping and tourist attraction, catering for visitors from all over the world. This brings many benefits but also a number of challenges, especially incorporating new buildings into a historic environment.

Travelodge in Windsor is modern but imposing.

Windsor Dials, a modern office development integrated into historic Windsor.

50. Riverside Apartments, Windsor

In 2019, Windsor and Eton are incredibly popular places to live. Educational standards are very high, and the proximity to Heathrow Airport and links to London make them very sought-after. Windsor is now probably best known for the four reasons: Windsor Castle, LEGOLAND, Eton College and, of course, royal weddings. Windsor attracts huge numbers of tourists every day, which certainly gives a buzz to the town with all the visiting nationalities. A royal home and fortress for over 900 years, the castle remains a working palace today. Not surprisingly Windsor and the surrounding areas contain some of the most expensive and desirable housing in the UK. As a place to live Windsor offers a wide variety of homes, from period cottages to elegant Georgian houses, Victorian terraces, thirties and more modern houses plus modern riverside flats.

The most expensive house currently for sale in 2019 was The Priory in Church Road, Old Windsor, an eight-bedroom listed eighteenth-century home, at £4.45 million.

Riverside apartments, a modern addition and incredibly expensive.

In St Leonard's Hill, a private road south of the town centre, North Lodge has six bedrooms and was on the market for £2.7 million (2019). The favoured 'golden triangle' sits between King's Road and Frances Road, adjacent to the Long Walk. A four-bedroom listed Georgian house here is £1.575 million (2019).

Affordable housing provision continues to be a challenge for the local authority as well as the integration of modern buildings into a primarily historic environment.

Bibliography

Farrar, Henry, *Windsor: Town and Castle* (Phillimore, 1990)
Fielder, Andrew, *Windsor, Eton and the Neighbourhood: A Visitor's Guide* (2011)
Friends of Windsor and Royal Museum, *Windsor Through Time* (Amberley Publishing, 2013)
Hill, B. J. W., *Windsor & Eton* (B.T. Batsford Ltd, 1957)
Home, Beatrice, *Windsor & Eton* (Adam & Charles Black, 1911)
Keenan, Debbie, *Windsor: A History and Celebration of the Town – The Francis Frith Collection* (Frith/Ottakars, 2004)
Macnaghten, Angus, *Windsor & Eton in Georgian Times* (1976)
Maple, Les, *Windsor: A Photographic History of Your Town* (Blackhorse Books, 2002)
Morriss, Richard K., *The Buildings of Windsor* (Alan Sutton Publishing Ltd, 1994)
Pevsner, Nikolaus, *The Buildings of England: Berkshire* (Penguin Books, 1993)
Robinson, J. M. *Windsor Castle: The Official Illustrated History* (Royal Collection Trust, 2017)
Rooney, Sheila, *Windsor & Eton: Centuries of Change* (Breedon Books Publishing, 2002)
South, R., *The Book of Windsor: The Story of a Royal Town* (Barracuda Books, 1977)
Stiles, Michael, *Around Windsor & Eton* (Sutton Publishing, 2004)
Windsor Local History Publications Group, *Windsor A Thousand Years: A Living History* (2001)
Windsor Local History Publications Group, *Streets of Windsor and Eton* (2004)
www.thamesweb.co.uk

Acknowledgements

Paul would like to thank his co-author Rob, who he has known since the fun days of Sheffield City Polytechnic (now Hallam University) while attempting to study Geography. Always fun when catching up.

Rob would like to thank his old room-mate Paul for the chance to be involved in this thoroughly enjoyable project.

About the Authors

Paul Rabbitts is a Fellow of the Royal Society of Arts, a Fellow of the Landscape Institute, currently Head of Parks at Watford Borough Council and is the author of over sixteen books, ranging from the history of public parks and the royal parks to the iconic Victorian bandstand, and has also written a number of books on architecture, including books from the *50 Buildings* series on Watford, Leighton Buzzard, Luton, Bournemouth, Salford and Manchester.

Rob Ickinger has lived in the Windsor area for eighteen years. He loves the town not only for its varied architecture but also for its close proximity to the Thames and Windsor Great Park, where he spends much of his time. Rob has a BA Hons in Geography from Sheffield Hallam University and has worked in the aviation industry for the past thirty years.